BRITTEN
AN EXTRAORDINARY LIFE

CHRISTOPHER MARK

ABRSM

First published in 2013 by ABRSM Publishing Ltd, a wholly owned subsidiary of ABRSM,
24 Portland Place, London W1B 1LU, United Kingdom

© 2013 by The Associated Board of the Royal Schools of Music

ISBN 978 1 84849 572 2

AB 3703

A CIP catalogue for this book is available from The British Library.
Design and formatting by www.9thplanetdesign.com
Typeset by Hope Services (Abingdon) Ltd, England
Printed in England by Caligraving Ltd, Thetford, Norfolk

to Peter Evans, in admiration and gratitude

Contents

Acknowledgements

We are grateful to the following for permission to reproduce photographs and extracts from copyright works:

Images

Front cover
Britten leaning over the prow of a boat, 1940s–50s. Photographer unknown. Britten's signature. Courtesy of the Britten-Pears Foundation.

Title page
Informal portrait of Britten, late 1950s. Photographer unknown. Courtesy of the Britten-Pears Foundation.

Inside pages
1. The Britten family and friends take tea in the garden, early 1920s. Photographer unknown. Courtesy of the Britten-Pears Foundation.
2. Britten and Frank Bridge dressed for tennis, 1930. Photographer unknown. Courtesy of the Britten-Pears Foundation.
3. Britten reading by a river, c. 1929. Photographer unknown. Courtesy of the Britten-Pears Foundation.
4. Britten and Peter Pears at the piano, in Long Island, USA, 1939. By permission of akg-images.
5. Britten with W. H. Auden, 1941. Photographer unknown. Courtesy of the Britten-Pears Foundation.
6. 7 Middagh Street. By permission of the NYC municipal archives.
7. Production photograph of *Peter Grimes*, Prologue, 1945. Photographed by Angus McBean (MS Thr 581). © Harvard Theatre Collection, Houghton Library, Harvard University.
8. Britten skiing in Switzerland, 1947. © Hänssler, Zürich 1947. Courtesy of the Britten-Pears Foundation.
9. Britten in his Rolls Royce with the children of the original cast of *Let's Make an Opera*, 1949. By permission of the Hulton Archive/Getty Images.
10. Rehearsal of *The Rape of Lucretia*, Glyndebourne, 1946. By permission of the Guy Gravett Collection/ArenaPAL.
11. Britten and Peter Pears coming off a plane, Delhi, 1955. By permission of Topfoto/ArenaPAL.
12. Britten and Mstislav Rostropovich, 1964. By permission of Brian Seed/Lebrecht Music & Arts.
13. Britten in Coventry Cathedral, 30 May 1962. By permission of Picture Post/Getty Images.
14. Britten in his office in the Red House, 1964. By permission of Brian Seed/Lebrecht Music & Arts.
15. Britten escorts HM Queen Elizabeth II at the opening of Snape Maltings, 2 June 1967. By permission of Brian Seed/Lebrecht Music & Arts.
16. Britten conducting at the Proms, mid-1960s. By permission of G. MacDomnic/Lebrecht Music & Arts.
17. Production photograph of *Death in Venice* at the Metropolitan Opera, New York, 1974. © Victor Parker 1974. Courtesy of the Britten-Pears Foundation.
18. Britten on his last holiday, near Bergen, Norway, 1976. © Rita Thomson 1976. Courtesy of the Britten-Pears Foundation.
19. Snape Maltings, 2004. © Chloë March.
20. The 50 pence coin commemorating the centenary of Britten's birth. With kind permission of the Royal Mint.

Text

The Letters and all other writings by Benjamin Britten and by Peter Pears are © the Britten-Pears Foundation.

Remembering Britten by Alan Blyth. © Alan Blyth, 1981. Reprinted by permission of A. M. Heath & Co. Ltd.

The Rape of Lucretia, libretto by Ronald Duncan. © 1946, 1947 by Hawkes & Son (London) Ltd. Reproduced by permission of Boosey & Hawkes Music Publishers Ltd.

Benjamin Britten: A Biography by Humphrey Carpenter. © The Estate of Humphrey Carpenter and reprinted by permission of Faber & Faber Ltd and the Estate of Humphrey Carpenter.

Britten's Children by John Bridcut. © John Bridcut and reprinted by permission of Faber & Faber Ltd.

Selected Letters of Michael Tippett edited by Thomas Schuttenhelm. © The Estate of Michael Tippett and reprinted by permission of Faber & Faber Ltd.

Introduction: 'To be useful, and to the living', from *On Receiving the First Aspen Award* by Benjamin Britten. Text © Faber Music Ltd, London. Reproduced by permission of the publishers. All rights reserved.

Paul Bunyan, text by Wystan Auden. © Faber Music Ltd, London. Reproduced by permission of the publishers. All rights reserved.

Death In Venice, libretto by Myfanwy Piper (based on the short story by Thomas Mann). © Faber Music Ltd, London. Reproduced by permission of the publishers. All rights reserved.

On Music: Essays and Diversions by Robin Holloway. Reproduced by permission of the author.

'Tippett and the Retreat from Mythology' by Derrick Puffett, from *The Musical Times*, 136 (Jan. 2001). By permission of The Musical Times Publications Ltd.

Obituary of Britten by Stanley Sadie, from *The Musical Times*, vol. 118, no. 1608 (Feb. 1977). By permission of The Musical Times Publications Ltd.

'Britten Returns to Composing' by Alan Blyth from *The Times*, 30 Dec. 1974. By permission of News Syndication.

Obituary: 'Lord Britten: a Major Contribution to English Music' from *The Times*, 6 Dec. 1976. By permission of News Syndication.

New Grove Dictionary of Music and Musicians (online edition) edited by Deane Root (2013). By permission of Oxford University Press.

Selling Britten by Paul Kildea. By permission of Oxford University Press.

The Music of Benjamin Britten by Peter Evans. By permission of Oxford University Press.

The Oxford History of Western Music, Vol. 3: Music in the Nineteenth Century by Richard Taruskin. By permission of Oxford University Press USA.

Those Twentieth Century Blues: An Autobiography by Michael Tippett, published by Hutchinson. Reprinted by permission of The Random House Group Ltd.

February House by Sheryl Tippins. © 2005 by Sheryl Tippins. Reprinted by permission of Ross Yoon Agency and Houghton Mifflin Harcourt Publishing Co. All rights reserved.

The Twentieth Century in Poetry: A Critical Survey by Peter Childs. By permission of Taylor & Francis Books (UK).

Music and Sexuality in Britten by Philip Brett. By permission of the University of California Press.

Preface

All present-day Britten scholars are in debt to various documentary enterprises initiated in the wake of the opening of the Britten archive at The Britten-Pears Library (BPL) in 1980. While Donald Mitchell did not complete the 'official' biography that Britten sanctioned, a good deal of the documentation he assembled with the help of the staff of the BPL informed Humphrey Carpenter's biography of 1992, *Benjamin Britten: A Biography*. Despite some significant flaws – the over-reliance on gossip as testimony, the over-eagerness to view the composer's music as an accurate reflection of the tensions in his life, the tendency to suppress the possibility that Britten might have been happy for at least some moments of his life – Carpenter's book has remained the essential point of reference for subsequent work. Mitchell was also the guiding hand behind the six volumes of Britten's letters (*Letters from a Life*) that have been published since 1991, the final volume appearing just before Britten's centenary year, 2013. These provide much of the raw material that Carpenter himself drew upon.

Among the copious editorial annotations in these volumes are quotations from the diaries that Britten kept from 1928 to 1938. The Britten Estate always intended that these should at some stage be published separately, and this finally happened in 2009, when *Journeying Boy: The Diaries of the Young Benjamin Britten 1928–1938* appeared under the Faber & Faber imprint, selected and edited by the one-time research scholar at the BPL, John Evans.

I quote a good deal from Britten's own words, and it will be evident that I owe much to *Journeying Boy* for this, as well as the various volumes of *Letters from a Life* and Paul Kildea's invaluable collection of Britten's writings in *Britten on Music*. A particular mention should be made of John Bridcut's book *Britten's Children*, his very thorough and sensitive exploration of a difficult aspect of Britten's life, which forms the main source for my inter-chapter entitled 'Boys' – though, as I indicate there, Bridcut also can be too willing to accept testimony as factual record and be reluctant to raise the possibility that (for understandable reasons) the whole story might not be being told.

I am also – again, like all Britten scholars – indebted to the BPL and its highly knowledgeable staff for their help during my visits over the past three decades, but especially during my examination for this book of Britten's later correspondence, at that time not published. I am very grateful to Mervyn Cooke and other experts for their feedback on drafts of the book, and to my wife, Chloë, and Ann Stott for their comments and support. My thanks, too, to Robin Barry for his sage advice and enthusiasm throughout the lifespan of this project, and to Ingalo Thomson for her judicious editing. The letters and all other writings by Benjamin Britten and Peter Pears are © The Britten-Pears Foundation, and I am grateful for the permission of the Trustees to reproduce them here.

As in the previous books in the *Extraordinary Life* series, the main text has four 'inter-chapters' placed within it. These step outside the main narrative and provide snapshots of aspects of Britten's life that can be said to have had particular significance, and which have relevance for more than just a short period. The placing of the inter-chapters shouldn't be regarded as arbitrary, and they sometimes cross-reference the main text, but they can also be read as 'stand-alone' items.

ABBREVIATIONS

In order to minimize clutter, I have employed abbreviations in the case of heavily used citations. These are:

BB   Humphrey Carpenter, *Benjamin Britten: A Biography* (London: Faber & Faber, 1992).

BBGO   Philip Brett, et al., 'Britten, Benjamin', in *Grove Music Online*, http:// www.oxfordmusiconline.com/subscriber/article/grove/music/46435

BC   John Bridcut, *Britten's Children* (London: Faber & Faber, 2006).

BoM   Paul Kildea (ed.), *Britten on Music* (New York: Oxford University Press, 2003).

BPL   a letter in the Britten-Pears Library that, at the time of writing, was unpublished.

JB   John Evans (ed.), *Journeying Boy: The Diaries of the Young Benjamin Britten 1928–1938* (London: Faber & Faber, 2009).

LL   the various volumes of *Letters from a Life* (labelled LL1, LL2, etc.):
        Donald Mitchell and Philip Reed (eds.), *Letters from a Life: Selected Diaries and Letters of Benjamin Britten. Volume 1 1923–39* (London: Faber & Faber, 1991).
        —— (eds.), *Letters from a Life: Selected Letters and Diaries of Benjamin Britten. Volume 2 1939–45* (London: Faber & Faber, 1991).

Donald Mitchell, Philip Reed and Mervyn Cooke (eds.), *Letters from a Life: Selected Letters of Benjamin Britten. Volume 3 1946–51* (London: Faber & Faber, 2004).

Philip Reed, Mervyn Cooke and Donald Mitchell (eds.), *Letters from a Life: Selected Letters of Benjamin Britten. Volume 4 1952–1957* (Woodbridge: Boydell Press, 2008).

Philip Reed and Mervyn Cooke (eds.), *Letters from a Life: The Selected Letters of Benjamin Britten. Volume 5 1958–1965* (Woodbridge: Boydell Press, 2010).

——(eds.), *Letters from a Life: The Selected Letters of Benjamin Britten. Volume 6 1966–1976* (Woodbridge: Boydell Press, 2012).

SB   Paul Kildea, *Selling Britten* (Oxford: Oxford University Press, 2002).

Citations for quotations from Britten's letters, diaries and published writings are normally followed by a reference in brackets in the main text; citations of the words of others occur in footnotes. Where several quotations from one volume of letters or the diaries occur in one paragraph, the source is identified the first time and page references only thereafter. Britten's spelling and punctuation could often veer from what is conventionally accepted, and in his letters and diaries I have kept the original, including the crossings-out that often accompanied the attempts to get the word right. [*Sic*] has been added to identify errors only in Britten's later published writings or in the words of others.

Christopher Mark
University of Surrey

INTRODUCTION:
'To be useful, and to the living'

Britten's very being seems to have been bound up with composition almost from birth. His diaries, which he started to keep in his fourteenth year, are full of matter-of-fact statements about what seems, to the rest of us, to be staggeringly copious composing, as if it were an entirely natural activity for someone of his age – which to him it obviously was. Later in life he formed various other interests – in the other arts, in playing sport and swimming (both started in childhood), driving top-of-the-range cars rather fast – but it was through composition that he defined himself and how others defined him. It is not unusual, of course, for a musician to be so consumed by his or her art. It was unusual, though, for a Briton of that era to arrive at music college – in Britten's case, the Royal College of Music in London – determined to make a career as a dedicated composer. That he should have entered the institution manifestly possessing the equipment to achieve his goal is one way in which he can be counted as extraordinary.

But was his life extraordinary? In his review of Humphrey Carpenter's biography of the composer, the most extensive biography published before 2013, Robin Holloway, a particularly insightful commentator on Britten, observes that, with the exception of 'dangerous livers like Berlioz or Wagner', most composers spend their lives 'entirely in writing music, playing music, making music happen; in some instances, they only fully come to life within music's domain and are incomplete human beings without it. They have no biography, let alone one of nearly six hundred pages'.[1] Holloway is obviously not saying that a biography of a composer, or one of Britten in particular, is pointless: it is a question of where the emphases lie. Calling for an 'intellectual biography more broadly interpreted

---

[1] Robin Holloway, *On Music: Essays and Diversions* (Brinkworth: Claridge Press, 2003), 211–12.

– "the growth of a poet's mind"', he sees these questions as being of the greatest moment as far as Britten is concerned: 'How was the sensibility formed? Whence the aesthetic of essentiality, the insistence on technical prowess, in a land of heartiness and amateurism? How did the Mahler/Berg nexus so important from so early receive its ideal home in this gauche product of a dowdy seaside resort and an English public school?' I broadly agree with Holloway, but to deliver fully what he sees as desirable would require a larger book than is my brief. Though I do attempt to incorporate some of the approaches he suggests, the aim of what follows is more modest: to sketch for the listener and concert-goer who may have read little about Britten a context that might afford a fuller understanding of his artistic motivations and decisions.

The biographically oriented literature on Britten is already substantial. In addition to the list of publications found in the Preface there is a volume of essays by (generally) younger scholars, some of which are biographical in scope, and a collection of essays by the late Philip Brett, whose bringing of Britten's sexuality into the discourse has given new insights into his artistic motivation and encouraged a hermeneutic approach in Britten studies.[2] Meanwhile the diaries Imogen Holst kept while she was Britten's amanuensis in the 1950s have been published in a recent book about her, and provide insights into his work patterns and more besides.[3] I have attempted to draw together what I have viewed as the most telling aspects of this research, and to offer – as one of my fellow contributors to this series has put it – a 'one-stop source on the man and his music'.[4] Inevitably, though, much of interest and importance has been left out, and I make no claims to omniscience in matters of interpretation. So I hope that this book will encourage readers to pursue aspects of special interest to them in the literature I have drawn upon.[5]

The main topics and issues of this book will not, in themselves, be news to anyone who has encountered Britten before. The directly musical topics include his complex relationship with modernism and the avant-garde, the various influences on his style, his choice of operatic subjects and poets, his performing activities, and so on. Non-musical topics that have a bearing on the kind of music he wrote include his homosexuality, his relationship with boys, his left-wing politics, his pacifism, his contact with various writers and artists, and his relationship with the Establishment (both court and musical). Other themes, too, will be introduced as the

---

[2] Lucy Walker (ed.), *Benjamin Britten: New Perspectives on his Life and Work* (Woodbridge: Boydell Press, 2009) and Philip Brett, *Music and Sexuality in Britten* (Berkeley, CA: University of California Press, 2006).

[3] Christopher Grogan (ed.), *Imogen Holst: A Life in Music* (Woodbridge: Boydell Press, 2007).

[4] J. P. E. Harper-Scott, *Elgar: An Extraordinary Life* (London: ABRSM, 2007), iv.

[5] Two other biographies – Paul Kildea, *Benjamin Britten: A Life in the Twentieth Century* (London: Allen Lane, 2013) and Neil Powell, *Benjamin Britten: A Life for Music* (London: Hutchinson, 2013) – were published too far into this book's publication process for me to take account of them.

book progresses. But the anchoring theme – the theme that I think is the best 'way in' to understanding what Britten is essentially about – is his view of the role of the composer in society, and the consequences of this for his artistic and technical development and the choices he made about how to live his life. A gathering of quotations shows clearly how he saw that role:[6]

From 'On Receiving the First Aspen Award' (1964)

I certainly write music for human beings – directly and deliberately … (256)

… it is the composer's duty, as a member of society, to speak to or for his fellow human beings. (257)

Music does not exist in a vacuum, it does not exist until it is performed, and performance imposes conditions. It is the easiest thing in the world to write a piece virtually or totally impossible to perform – but oddly enough that is not what I prefer to do; I prefer to study the conditions of performance and shape my music to them. (257)

… it is quite a good thing to please people, even if only for today. That is what we should aim at – pleasing people today as seriously as we can, and letting the future look after itself. (259)

… a musical experience needs three human beings at least. It requires a composer, a performer, and a listener; and unless these three take part together there is no musical experience. (261)

I write music, now, in Aldeburgh, for people living there, and further afield, indeed for anyone who cares to play it or listen to it. But my music now has its roots, in where I live and work. (262)

From 'Tribute to Michael Tippett' (1965)

What matters to us now is that people want to use our music. For that, as I see it, is our job – to be useful, and to the living. (274)

These quotations come from just two of numerous interviews, speeches and essays from the 1960s, during which period Britten's view of himself as an Establishment figure (qualified though this had to be because of the various ways in which he was marked as an outsider) grew to its greatest extent. It was also the period in which he became most concerned about the threat to a fully functioning musical culture from what he saw as an increasing disconnection between audiences and contemporary composers. Many quotations on this matter could be assembled at this point, and two follow below. The first is from a speech given on receiving an honorary degree from the University of Hull: 'The craze for originality, one result of the nineteenth century cult of personality, has driven many artists into using

---

[6] Each quotation is sourced from *BoM*; its page number appears at the end of the quotation.

a language to which very few hold the key, and that is a pity. To use a language which can be understood is an advantage, not a disadvantage' (215). The second is on the subject of the technical device perhaps most associated with the avant-garde:

> I find [the twelve-tone system] has jettisoned too many devices that I wish to retains [sic]: key centres, melodic & rhythmic patterns, for instance. Without these I find it impossible to vary the tensions of my music ... But this is not to say that other composers need the devices I do, but my guess is that a lack of these devices may have helped to cause the well-known gap between contemporary music & the general public – because of a sense of bewilderment or boredom caused by lack of perceptible design. (239)

Britten's views on the relationship between the composer and society are linked to his humanitarianism and his political stance – though left-wing sympathies are no guarantee of composing the sort of music that Britten saw as likely to connect with a broad public (he would have viewed the communist Luigi Nono as an 'Ivory Tower' composer, for example[7]). Naturally he was also mindful of what kind of music he had to write if he was to earn his living as a composer; clearly, it had to engage the public, fulfil the needs of administrators, and stimulate the people he hoped would sing and play it. But Britten was not simply a community musician. It would be odd if particularly gifted composers did not wish to explore their abilities to the limit, and this would almost certainly involve at some stage writing for cognoscenti. Sometimes it is possible to write for a broad audience and cognoscenti at the same time (as Mozart famously noted), and one of the features that makes Britten's music unusual in the mid- to late twentieth century is his ability to do this. But there are a number of works, particularly from the 1960s, in which he seems to withdraw from the public gaze. It is in these works that he most fully explores adaptations of various developments associated with the avant-garde; some of these developments, however, also had a significant influence at the beginning of his career, and might, if circumstances had been different, have taken him in a different direction.

---

[7] Nono had such a low opinion of Britten's music in 1959 that he refused to meet him at the Dartington Summer School that year (see BB 459), though they dined together in Venice in 1962 and the event seems to have been very cordial (see Britten's letter to Nono in LL5 438).

ONE

SETTING OUT (1913–1939)

Benjamin Britten's first words in his diary for Friday 23 February 1934, written above the date itself, suggesting they were added later, read simply: 'Elgar dies' (*JB* 200–201). But that day Britten was more concerned with birth than with the passing of a composer whom he then disliked with some intensity. For in the evening he attended the first performance of his own choral variations, *A Boy was Born*, Op. 3 (1933), in a BBC 'Concert of Contemporary Music'.

Even though his Opp. 1 and 2 – the Sinfonietta for chamber orchestra and the Phantasy for oboe and string trio, both composed in 1932 – had already been performed, Britten's Op. 3 is more ambitious and as long (at around thirty minutes) as the two other works combined. Part of the ambition is indeed in the length, for it is difficult to maintain a sense of a continuing span over half an hour or so of unaccompanied singing, especially when the text, which Britten selected from Edith Rickert's collection, *Ancient English Christmas Carols*,[1] provides such a diversity of images (there are six variations, one of which uses two different texts, and one – the finale – four). Even when the variations are relatively self-contained, as is the case with the third, 'Jesu, as Thou art our Saviour', the impression is still conveyed that they are part of a greater whole. This is partly brought about by the relatively 'weak' cadence or simple fade-out at the end of each variation, but it also results from carefully plotted changes in scale-content from one variation to the next, so that the work is integrated by one overarching process. Also ambitious is the derivation of virtually all the melodic material from one three-note package, the first three notes sung by the sopranos; to achieve sufficient variety in these circumstances requires a level of technique approaching the virtuosic, as well as considerable confidence. The most obvious intimation of the mature

---

[1] Edith Rickert (ed.), *Ancient English Carols 1400–1700* (London: Chatto and Windus, 1910; repr. 1914, 1928).

Britten, however, lies in his setting of words, for which he already had a formidable facility, and in the precision and imagination of his sonorous imagery (one example being the invocation of freezing cold through the biting semitonal clashes in the fifth variation, 'In the Bleak Mid-Winter'). While it would be wrong to say that Britten had sprung into public view fully formed, it could be argued that the essence of his musical personality can be heard in this, his first work to receive a wide hearing.

On the day that *A Boy was Born* was first performed, Britten had been a student at the Royal College of Music (RCM) for three years and five months, having entered in September 1930. It had taken him considerably less time than Elgar not only to make Britain's musical capital his base, but also, in having his music broadcast by the BBC, to acquire a national audience. Elgar didn't move to London until 1889, when he was 32, but retreated to the Malverns a couple of years later after failing to establish himself; only in the late 1890s, by the time he was known nationally, did he begin to have some London success.

So what guided Britten from a childhood in a rather ordinary, provincial middle-class family towards this remarkable achievement? Within this biography certain themes that are key to understanding his artistic persona will be seen to emerge. Many of these can be expressed as oppositions: haven versus threat; confidence versus doubt; home versus away; closed versus open; physical exuberance (sport) versus physical tentativeness (sex). Beginning the narrative is a version of the first on this list, innocence and its imperilling – the Britten topos that has been most widely recognized and discussed.

'One curious thing about this boy'

Much of Britten's music revolves around the theme of corrupted innocence. Often, though by no means always, it is childhood innocence that is imperilled, so commentators perhaps unsurprisingly have looked for a source for this within Britten's early years in Lowestoft, Suffolk, the most easterly town in the UK, where he was born on 22 November 1913. During research for his biography Humphrey Carpenter found suggestions of a particularly dark episode. Eric Crozier, who collaborated with Britten as opera producer and librettist, stated in a memoir that the composer had told him in the late 1940s that he 'had been raped by a master at his school'. Crozier could recall no further details, but he believed Britten was offering this as an explanation for his homosexuality.[2] Britten also mentioned to a member of the Mayer family, with whom he stayed during his years in North America (1939–42), that 'very traumatic experiences, sexual experiences' occurred during his childhood. But other friends

---

[2] *BB* 20.

interviewed by Carpenter were sceptical of Crozier's story,[3] and it is impossible to determine the veracity of it, or of the statement Britten allegedly made to another of his librettists, Myfanwy Piper, that 'his father was homosexual and that he used to send him out to find boys ... not meaning to go to the street corners and see a pretty errand boy, but "Why don't you bring your pals home from school?"'.[4] Carpenter asks if they weren't both 'fantasies on Britten's part, sparked off while his imagination was at work on his operas'.[5]

If Britten's story about his father, Robert, were indeed fantasy, two of his siblings – his brother, also called Robert, and the younger of his two sisters, Beth (the older sister was Barbara; Benjamin was the youngest) – nevertheless asserted during the filming of Tony Palmer's 1979 documentary about Britten[6] that their childhood home life was far from untroubled. Interviewed by Carpenter, Palmer recounted that Beth, off the record, 'had let slip that it was not actually a terribly happy family atmosphere', and, when questioned on this before filming, Robert junior had said, 'We liked our mother, but we were a bit afraid of our father ... My sisters and I thought my father had funny habits.' Quite what these 'funny habits' were is unknown, though the reference might be to drinking habits.[7] Fondness for alcohol was a family trait: one of Robert senior's brothers died from excessive intake. With the other brother ruining the family business,[8] it is not surprising that Britten's father, a well-respected dentist, should seek out trappings of social conventionality and acceptability such as membership of the Lowestoft yacht club.

The negativity of Britten's remark to Myfanwy Piper regarding his father is, however, offset by his comment in late 1963 to his friend Ronald Duncan (also *The Rape of Lucretia*'s librettist) in response to reading Duncan's autobiography; it included a story related to him by Britten about his father's difficulty in talking to him about sex before he went to boarding school: 'The story about my father rather hurts me – it makes him out to be rather a fool, instead of the intelligent sympathetic man he was – although like most parents of that generation tongue-tied in coping with that particular subject (as you rightly say)' (*LL5* 516). And on his father's death he wrote in his diary: 'A great man – with one of the finest brains I have ever come across, & what a father!' (*JB* 207).

There were skeletons on Britten's mother's side of the closet as well. She was at pains to hide her own family history, removing genealogical entries from the family bible and apparently only admitting that her father had

[3] *BB* 20.
[4] *BB* 23.
[5] *BB* 25.
[6] *A Time There Was*, 1979; digitally restored and released on DVD in November 2006.
[7] *BB* 24.
[8] *BB* 4.

1. The Britten family and friends take tea in the garden, in the early 1920s. From left to right: Britten's father, Robert Britten; his mother, Edith Britten, with his younger sister Beth sitting in front of her; Britten himself; and two unidentified girls.

been illegitimate under questioning from her younger daughter.[9] Britten, too, was to find it necessary to employ secrecy and misdirection, and to wear a cloak of middle-class respectability (actually, a tighter-fitting garment than that), hanging in a different metaphorical closet.

It was not unusual in early twentieth-century middle-class English households for the father to be distant and stern and the mother to be a little warmer and nurturing (even when, as in the Brittens' case, aspects of maternal caring were delegated to a nanny and the meals prepared by a cook). Britten's father fitted the traditional role, down to having his own chair in the living room that no one else would dare sit in.[10] Britten's mother, especially protective of her youngest child since a bout of pneumonia at three months old nearly led to his death, was the driving force behind his initial musical development. An amateur soprano and member of the Lowestoft Musical Society, she arranged piano and theory lessons for him with one of her contacts, Ethel Astle, a local teacher. Mrs Britten created a home musical environment that revolved around her talented son, ensuring that he had priority on the piano and that he was the focus (as soloist, duet partner, and accompanist) of the musical evenings that took place in their home. One of Britten's school friends, Basil Reeve, went so far as to suggest that his mother strictly controlled all of his activity when he was at home and 'was *determined* that he should be a great musician'. Apparently she was entirely confident that he would be 'the fourth B' – 'The three Bs were Bach, Beethoven and Brahms, and the fourth B was Britten.'[11] There is no extant comment from Britten about his mother's role in his musical education; certainly there is no complaint at being worked hard by her. Indeed it is clear from his letters that there was an extraordinarily close relationship between them.

The Brittens' musical evenings took place in their first-floor drawing room, which was nicknamed 'Heaven' by Britten's father because it was his upstairs refuge from his ground-floor surgery. Whatever the other delights of Britten's early childhood, his being in 'Heaven' exercising the gifts he surely knew were prodigious in front of an adoring audience must have been idyllic, and certainly in retrospect: it was his removal from home and incarceration at boarding school in 1928 that instilled his first strong feelings of alienation and loss. Being bundled off to a strange place with strange rules was not out of the ordinary for a middle-class English boy of that time, but Britten seems to have reacted with unusual intensity.

As was the custom, he was introduced to some of those rules at a preparatory school, South Lodge, which he attended from 1923 to 1928 as

---

[9] *BB* 4.
[10] See *BB* 8: 'When Marjorie [Goldson, who was to become Robert Britten's wife] ... sat down in a chair in the drawing-room, and faces fell: "Oh, not *there*, that's Pop's chair."'
[11] Interview with Donald Mitchell quoted in Mitchell's 'Introduction' to *LL*1 11–12. See also extracts from John Bridcut's interview with Reeve, *BC* 9.

a dayboy. Transgression of the rules could sometimes lead to beatings, and he wondered many years later whether this led to his lifelong, passionate pacifism.[12] South Lodge was far from being continuous sufferance, however. It was here that one of the most important aspects of his life took hold. If there was any activity that stood a chance of rivalling music in Britten's passions, it was sport – all the more so because he was very good at it. His passion for cricket burgeoned during his time at his prep school, where he was captain of the XI in his final term and elected *victor ludorum* for his all-round sporting prowess. Later, at his public school, Gresham's in Holt, he added hockey and tennis. Throughout most of his life he enjoyed racket sports, taking up squash on 13 March 1937 (his diary entry for that day states that 'Peter [Burra] initiates me into the wonders of Squash which I find completely captivating & I curse myself for not having played it before' (*JB* 418)). In his early twenties he took up surfing off the Cornwall coast, to the extent that, on 26 July 1936, he felt he could boast to himself 'I am becoming the complete surfist now' (365); writing to his mother two days later he confessed: 'And as for surfing you will go dotty over it – there is nothing like it in the world' (*LL1* 436). Surfing supplemented the swimming (or bathing, as he called it) that seems at times to have been almost an addiction, possibly as a result of being born so close to sea. His quest for physical exhilaration also drew him to skiing in Switzerland in the late 1940s,[13] and one way he tried to deal with depression during his stay in the United States was to drive a borrowed car very fast along a beach.[14]

While South Lodge could be put behind him at the end of the day, this was of course not possible at Gresham's, and the 14-year-old Britten's first reactions to the school, recorded in the diary he began on his first day there, Thursday 20 September 1928, are full of foreboding: 'Mummy, Daddy, and Bobby, take me to Holt, to school, worse luck!' The second day was not an improvement: 'We do ~~are~~ our Studies (I am in a study 3 boys, who might be worse, but might be better. They are full of swearing and vulgarity), in the morning, and have chapel at 10.30. Work in the afternoon. Bed at 9.30. I do not like the outlook of 13 weeks of this!' (*JB* 13). Indeed, his diaries chronicle a portfolio of negative emotional states throughout his time at Gresham's:

> *Terror*
> I really think that last night was the most miserable night, of my existance. 1. I couldn't get to sleep (not. unusual). 2. I had litterally about 6 terrible dreams, seperated by about ½ hr of sleeplessness. In 1. Mummy was killed by a chimney stack falling through the roof.

---

[12] He describes witnessing a beating in an interview in the *Guardian*, 7 June 1971.
[13] *LL3* 285.
[14] John Bridcut, *The Faber Pocket Guide to Britten* (London: Faber & Faber, 2010), 139.

2. Pop was killed when driving a bus (!) over Kessingland dam.
3. Beth (or Barbara) was burned in the house catching fire. I cannot remember the others. (*JB* 31)

Loneliness
I do detest leaving home, there is that utter loneliness at school, which I loathe. (14)

How I loathe this abominable hole. I am still in the Biddyhole, with the most impossible crowd. I simply cannot see how I can bare up through it, & suicide is so cowardly. Running away's as bad; so I suppose I've got to stick it. But 83 days! (29)

Boredom
I am frightfully bored really, because there is so little to-do. Music is the only thing – what I should do without it, God only knows; but even that you cannot do always in a place full of rowdy, inquisitive ("what's that you've got there") boys. (33–4)

To add to his woes, he was often ill, spending numerous days in the school sanatorium or confined to his bed at home. And he was particularly dismayed by what he saw as the institutional quashing of creativity: 'Originality (oh! that blessed thing) is completely discouraged. If you are original, well you are considered a lunatic, & consequently become unpopular. Unpopularity is then a thing to be aimed for in Gresham's School Holt then' (*JB* 26–7).

It is impossible to know the extent to which Britten is overdramatizing, but the general impression given by the diaries is of getting through each term by the gritting of teeth. Despite this, his consistent castigating of the standards of musical performance at the school, and worries about his academic work, he managed to confess on leaving that 'It is marvellous to be home, but I didn't think I should be so sorry to leave' (*JB* 39). He was more than simply respected as a musician and admits in the preface to *Simple Symphony*, Op. 4 (his 1934 reworking of some childhood pieces) that the 'one curious thing about this boy' – that 'he wrote music' – was tolerated: 'His friends bore with it, his enemies kicked a bit but not for long (he was quite tough), the staff couldn't object if his work and games didn't suffer' (*BoM* 358).

Britten finished his stretch at Gresham's in the summer of 1930, passing his School Certificate and gaining an open scholarship to the Royal College of Music in London. His relationship with institutions of learning would continue to be problematic, though, and much of what he seems to have regarded as his real musical education lay elsewhere. To an extent he educated himself through listening to the radio and to gramophone records, and studying scores. His acquisition of compositional craft, however, was largely directed by Frank Bridge (1879–1941), with whom Britten studied privately from the later months of 1927.

Bridge

Britten was introduced to Bridge by Audrey Alston, his viola teacher, but he already knew who he was, for he had been 'knocked sideways' by *The Sea* (1910–11) at the Norwich Triennial Festival in 1924. They first met after the first performance of Bridge's *Enter Spring* at the 1927 Festival.

Britten's article 'Britten Looking Back', published in the *Sunday Telegraph* just before his fiftieth birthday,[15] is a good gauge of how important Bridge was to him. Uncomfortable about the attention his birthday was receiving, Britten attempted to change the focus by writing entirely about his teacher. The emphasis is firmly on craft: 'I badly needed his kind of strictness; it was just the right treatment for me. His loathing of all sloppiness and amateurishness set me standards to aim for that I've never forgotten' (*BoM* 250–51). Britten insisted that he was hugely aware of not yet having achieved the technical standards set for him by Bridge, noting that 'In everything he did for me, there were perhaps above all two cardinal principles. One was that you should try to find yourself and be true to what you find. The other – obviously connected with it – was his scrupulous attention to technique, the business of saying clearly what was in one's mind' (253).

These are generalities: what about specifics? There are a few notations in Bridge's hand on the young composer's manuscripts, but not many, and while these were probably instructive for Britten, the most important feedback that he got from his lessons was oral and aural. Before coming under Bridge's guidance, Britten had written a large quantity of music in a wide variety of genres, employing the conventions of tonal and harmonic behaviour that underpin the repertory from Bach to Brahms (the so-called common-practice period).[16] One of the first works completed after his tutelage began, the *Quatre chansons françaises*, composed between 16 June and 31 August 1928, is more adventurous, however. It draws on traits of not only Ravel and Debussy, but also Wagner, and Arnold Schoenberg's pupil Alban Berg: the ending of the work is almost a quotation of the final bars of Wagner's *Tristan und Isolde*, and some of the chords employed in the first song resemble particularly significant chords in Berg's atonal first opera, *Wozzeck*. *Quatre chansons françaises* is notable too for the bitter irony of the third song, 'L'Enfance', which depicts a child innocently playing while his mother dies of consumption (an odd offering for Britten to make to his parents on the occasion of their wedding anniversary), and for its extraordinarily adept orchestration.

If some 'updating' came off Britten's own bat, thanks to his assiduous listening and score-reading, it is inconceivable that Bridge would not have pointed him towards the music which informed the radicalization of his

---

[15] Reproduced in *BoM* 250–53.
[16] I discuss Britten's juvenilia in detail in Christopher Mark, 'Juvenilia (1922–1932)', in Mervyn Cooke (ed.), *The Cambridge Companion to Benjamin Britten* (Cambridge: Cambridge University Press, 1999), 11–35.

2. Britten and Frank Bridge attired for tennis, 1930.

own work after the watershed Piano Sonata (1921–4) – in, for example, *There is a Willow Grows Aslant a Brook*, for viola and small orchestra (1928; Britten arranged this for viola and piano in December 1932), and *Oration, Concerto elegiaco*, for cello and orchestra (1930). The most insightful of Bridge commentators, the composer Anthony Payne, notes similarities to the early works of the Second Viennese School in Bridge's Third and Fourth String Quartets:

> There is the same determination to keep all 12 chromatic notes in play, the same pervasiveness of motivic relationships. Yet Bridge's essential Englishness is always somehow in evidence, particularly in his sensuous use of harmony, and although his admiration for Berg is often evident, his own personality remains strongly individual.[17]

Britten's own interest in Schoenberg is well documented in his diaries, especially at the time he was composing *Quartettino* (1930), which represents the furthest he was to go at any time during his student days or professional career towards Schoenberg's jettisoning of tonality. 7 April 1930, for example, sees him listening to 'a marvellous Schönberg concert' on the

[17] Anthony Payne, et al., 'Bridge, Frank', in *Grove Music Online* <http://www.oxfordmusiconline. com/subscriber/article/grove/music/48240>, accessed 3 April 2012.

radio which included what for many had become the *locus classicus* of atonality, *Pierrot lunaire* (*JB* 36). If the extended chromaticism Britten employed in *Quartettino* was short-lived, Schoenberg's intensive motivic working – a process by which melodic and harmonic material is generated from a small number of basic cells, or packages of notes – had a more lasting impact. Indeed, this type of working, already noted in *A Boy was Born*, would still be playing a central role in Britten's final opera.

It was inevitable that Britten would rebel, and this began soon after he started at music college: 'When Bridge played questionable chords across the room at me and asked if that was what I meant, I would retort, "Yes, it is." He'd grunt back, "Well it oughtn't to be"' (*BoM* 251). In fact, their closest point, compositionally speaking, had already come and gone in the *Quartettino*, after which Britten's music becomes more fundamentally diatonic – that is, it tends to employ as its basic material the familiar major and minor scales that had been in use for two centuries, albeit in often highly distinctive ways that bend or rewrite 'the rules' or substitute new ones. Bridge continued to advise Britten after he entered the RCM, but the younger composer was always going to need to carve out a clear space between himself and the man whom in 1930 he had declared to be 'England's premier composer' (*LL1* 143). Britten's diary and other documents show that, certainly by 1937, when he was firmly launched as a composer, he was seeking to do exactly this – as shown in his response to Bridge's Piano Trio No. 2 in mid-February:

> It is a fine work – genuinely musical & really inspired I feel. Perhaps a weakness is the restriction of harmonic & melodic language, which becomes a fraction tedious. It is as if a poet set out to write; & decided to avoid using the verb 'to be'. (This is of course 90% of the trouble of contemporary music). Even so, I feel this leaves every other bit of recent British (& most foreign) chamber-music standing. (*JB* 332)

In the next month he was again being critical of Bridge and, actually, a little patronizing: 'Grand Conversations – he is a fine thinker, but not so domineering as to prevent any observations from myself. I feel that he has a rather precious & escapist view of art – but that is typical of his generation – & eminently excusable. But his enthusiasm for music & his understanding of the classics is a tremendous virtue' (*JB* 413). In June and July Britten composed his Variations on a Theme of Frank Bridge, and while this is certainly a warm tribute to his former teacher, it is arguably an even stronger assertion of independence, creating a good deal of stylistic and expressive distance between Bridge's theme and his own brilliant treatment of it. By December 1937 relations had actually become fractious, as Bridge's friend Marjorie Fass reported: 'As Franco got out of his car he muttered to me that never again wld he try to help Benjy over his work, as some of the things he pointed out, the boy simply wldn't alter, so why waste his time & energy?'[18]

London

Britten's arrival at the RCM in September 1930 came at a good time for him to be in London, for a number of developments around then improved standards of performance and the range of music being performed.[19] That year, for example, the BBC Orchestra was established, with players placed on permanent contracts in a bid to boost the level of playing. In 1931 Anne Macnaghten, Iris Lemare, and Elisabeth Lutyens established the Macnaghten Concerts for the performance of contemporary music,[20] while in 1932 Thomas Beecham formed the London Philharmonic Orchestra (LPO). Britten benefited directly from the Macnaghten concerts (from 1932 renamed the Macnaghten-Lemare concerts). Between December 1932 and December 1934 six of his works, including the Sinfonietta, Op. 1, received their premiere, or the premiere of their revised version, under their auspices.[21] The BBC Orchestra gave the first broadcast of the Sinfonietta in December 1933, while the LPO gave the first performance a few years later of *Our Hunting Fathers*, Op. 8. Which isn't to say that Britten himself was always impressed by the standards of playing: hearing the BBC Orchestra under Toscanini in June 1935 he declared that, despite playing better than usual, 'even now it is not 1st class – sometimes not even capable' (*JB* 265).

As this comment might suggest, Britten's musical opinions were nothing if not certain. Strong likes and dislikes pepper his diaries and letters. He was still, at that stage, deeply committed to Beethoven, his childhood hero – the composer whom in 1928 he described as 'first, and I think always will be' (*JB* 14). As it turned out, the last sentiment was not to be the case (by 1963 he was finding the sound of Beethoven's Op. 111 Variations 'grotesque' (*BoM* 228)), but in the summer of 1936 he was still pouring over the later quartets with profit.[22] Another composer who figured large in his childhood listening and score-collecting was Wagner, whose *Siegfried Idyll* he used to play to his mother on the piano, reading from his miniature score.[23] He is the one composer about whom Britten's views are most consistently reverential. He attended a performance of the *Ring* cycle in May 1936, and despite his poor view of Beecham's conducting

---

[18] LL1 25.

[19] Nicholas Temperley, et al., 'London (i) §VI: Musical life: 1800–1945', in *Grove Music Online* <http://www.oxfordmusiconline.com/subscriber/article/grove/music/16904>, accessed 3 April 2012.

[20] See Anne Macnaghten's own account in *The Musical Times*, 100 (Sept. 1959), 460–61.

[21] The Sinfonietta received its premiere on 31 January 1933. The other works were: Phantasy in F minor for string quintet, December 1932; Three Two-Part Songs, 12 December 1932; Two Part-Songs and Alla Marcia for string quartet, 11 December 1933; *A Boy was Born*, first performance of revised version, 17 December 1934.

[22] JB 362.

[23] BC 10.

and the orchestra's playing, it was still 'a great priviledge going to this Ring' (*JB* 354): 'The Wagner fever is as strong as ever on me, but less hypnotic than before I hope. Now I more appreciate the colossal dramatic & musical skill, sheer invention in every direction' (356). In this period in British concert life, Mahler had nothing like the popularity he holds today, but he too made a big impression on Britten, receiving his first diary mention in the week Britten started at the RCM: 'Mahler 4th. Much too long, but beautiful in pts' (53). He records two further hearings of that work, both positive, with the Ninth Symphony also making a big impact: 'I could listen to this for hours' (245).

Of living contemporary composers apart from Bridge, Britten was most impressed by Schoenberg, Berg and Stravinsky. He was not entirely without reservations, though. Despite his enthusiasm for *Pierrot lunaire*, some of Schoenberg's music puzzled him – of *Ewartung*, which he heard in January 1931, he said, 'I could not make head or tail of it' (*JB* 60) – and some he was not so impressed by. The Variations for Orchestra, Op. 31, for example, he regarded in 1933 as 'dull', though with 'some good things in it' (130). And after a broadcast performance of Berg's 'astounding' *Lyric Suite* by the Kolisch Quartet in February 1933 he wrote that 'The imagination & intense emotion of this work certainly amaze me if not altogether pleases me' (131). The Violin Concerto, however, he seems to have embraced wholeheartedly: after attending the first performance in Barcelona in April 1936 he described it as 'just shattering – very simple, & touching' (348). Later that year he bought the score and after hearing another performance reported that it had 'an extremely moving effect on me like no other stuff' (393). Meanwhile, he noted that the *Wozzeck* pieces, which Berg extracted from his opera, 'always leave me like a wet rag' (348).

As for Stravinsky, Britten was not wholeheartedly drawn to the *Rite of Spring*, finding it in January 1931 'bewildering & terrifying. I didn't really enjoy it, but I think it's incredibly marvellous & arresting' (*JB* 62). He was rather more taken with the *Symphony of Psalms*, the first English performance of which he attended (on 16 November 1931), and which in September 1934 he describes as an 'incredible' masterpiece (223). This work is closer to Britten in both style and aesthetic, as is *Apollon Musagète*, which in 1935 he mentions as having 'some v. lovely things in it' (250). The leading Russian (or, rather, Soviet) of the next generation, Shostakovich, who was just emerging, is on the surface even more similar in outlook, and Britten's admiration for him is clear from the start: of the First Symphony, which he heard in March 1935, he wrote: '[it is] a miracle for a boy of 17, very uneven, but with some splendid imagination' (255).[24] Other individual works that made a strong impression include Kodály's *Psalmus hungaricus*, the score of

---

[24] It was in fact completed when Shostakovich was 19.

which Britten acquired in June 1932, and Bartók's *Miraculous Mandarin*, which he heard the previous March: 'I cannot say I <u>love</u> this music, but it is amazingly clever & descriptive' (101).

About contemporary English music he was more equivocal. He was initially attracted to some of Delius's work, finding *Sea Drift* 'v. beautiful' in 1933 (*JB* 130), but later that year commented that the new *Idyll* 'just says what D. has said so often before, & perhaps it doesn't say it as well' (150).[25] He wanted to admire Holst, but found it difficult: after listening to his memorial concert in June 1934 he wrote, ruefully, 'I wish I could think he was great!' (215). Of Bliss he was brazenly contemptuous, describing the Clarinet Quintet as 'V. unoriginal piffle & it wasn't even amusing, but intensely dull' (139).

Perhaps the most interesting response is to Walton. In his fiftieth year Britten wrote to the older composer:

> I don't know if I ever told you, but hearing your Viola Concerto & Portsmouth Point (works which I still love dearly) was a great turning point in my musical life. I'd got in a muddle; poor old John Ireland wasn't much help, & I couldn't get on with the 12-tone idea (still can't) – & you showed me the way of being relaxed and fresh, & intensely personal & yet still with the terms of reference which I had to have. It comes, I'm sure, because the ideas were fine & clear, which is all that matters … (*LL*1 202).

This was a reply to a generous tribute from Walton in which he said that Britten's music 'shines out as a beacon (how banal I'm becoming!) in, to me at least, a chaotic & barren musical world' (*LL*1 203). Of course, true feelings do not necessarily present themselves in written exchanges of pleasantries, but the evidence of Britten's diary is that his response to the Viola Concerto was warm: on a British Composers' Night at the Proms on 10 September 1931 it 'stood out as a work of genius' (*JB* 83). His opinion of a gramophone recording of *Portsmouth Point* in August 1932 was, however, nothing if not damning: 'Disappointed. Ineffective & apparently bad & careless workmanship' (113): there is not much sign here that 'the ideas were fine & clear'. The previous month he had described *Façade* as 'Delightful & attractive' (109), but he was increasingly finding things about Walton's music to criticize. In 1934, after rehearing *Belshazzar's Feast*, he wrote that 'there isn't quite enough left when the glitter & icing is taken away' (196). Walton's stock hit rock bottom with the first complete performance of the First Symphony in November 1935: this was 'A great tragedy for English music. Last hope of W. gone now – this is a conventional work, reactionery in the extreme & dull to a degree' (285). Four months later Britten spent 'hysterical evenings' with the

---

[25] Britten conducted Delius's *Summer Night on the River* in the first concert to take place at Snape Maltings.

composer Lennox Berkeley pulling the score to pieces, focusing on the 'abominable scoring' and 'over pretentiousness' (365).

Given all this, the degree of tension between Britten and Walton socially is not surprising: after lunch with him in July 1937 Britten described his senior as 'charming, but I feel always the school relationship with him – he is so obviously the head-prefect of English music, whereas I'm the promising young new boy' (*JB* 445). It must have been difficult for the much less fecund Walton to avoid feelings of jealousy and resentment as Britten's career developed and his own seemed to stall: his abilities were much more circumscribed, whatever the achievements of the Viola Concerto and (certainly in part) *Façade*, the First Symphony, and *Belshazzar's Feast*. His fiftieth-birthday tribute to Britten seems particularly generous in this context.

The other composer who got it in the neck during the 'hysterical evenings' with Berkeley was Vaughan Williams, whose Fourth Symphony was bracketed with Walton's First and found wanting in the same way; Britten in fact went further and tarred it with 'amateurishness & clumsiness' (*JB* 365). He thought the Tallis Fantasia 'V. beautiful (wonderfully scored), but over long' (72), and is equivocal about the Phantasy Quintet (it 'has some good things in it, but technically inefficient & imitative, & didn't seem to hang together' (138)), but these are the only comments with anything positive about them. He had already had a go at Vaughan Williams's Fourth Symphony in his diary before setting about it with Berkeley, having heard the '1st & I hope last perf.' in April 1935 (257), while *The Lark Ascending* was 'rambling & interminable', even when conducted by Bridge (288). In a 1959 interview he admitted that during his student days he was 'frankly suspicious of V.W. My struggle all the time was to develop a consciously controlled professional technique. It was a struggle away from everything Vaughan Williams seemed to stand for' (*BoM* 171). Remarkably, he told this interviewer that he had been much impressed by the Fourth Symphony, but it is difficult to see this as anything but a middle-aged massaging of the truth to avoid any unpleasantness. On Vaughan Williams's death in 1958 Britten wrote to his widow, Ursula, saying that her husband had 'been such a tremendous figure to me, all my musical life ... We will miss him sadly – above all, his wonderful, uncompromising courage in fighting for all those things he believed in – things which I personally believe to be some of the most important things in life' (*LL5* 69). This skilfully detaches the man from his music, but there seems no reason to doubt the authenticity of his tribute.

Britten's elaboration of the school-relationship analogy in English music identifies Vaughan Williams as 'of course the Headmaster'. Elgar, he goes on, 'was never that – but a member of the Governing Board' (*JB* 445). While Britten never really made his peace with Vaughan Williams's music (despite recording *On Wenlock Edge* in 1948), he did come round to Elgar in the late 1960s to the extent of recording both the Introduction and Allegro for strings and *The Dream of Gerontius*.[26] In the 1930s, though, he could see Elgar only as a figure to react against, going so far as to note in his diary in November 1935 that 'the best way to make me like Elgar is to listen to him after Vaughan Williams' (285). The Second Symphony he found to be 'dreadful (nobilmente sempre) – I come out after 3rd movement – <u>so</u> bored' (54), while 'only in Imperialist England would such a work [as the First Symphony] be tolerated' (276). In May 1931 one of his longest diary deliberations concerned the 'Enigma' Variations, which had come on the heels of Mahler's *Lieder eines fahrenden Gesellen* and provided 'a terrible contrast': 'I listened with an open mind, but cannot say that I was less annoyed by them, than usual' (72). He clearly felt, though, that Elgar possessed a quality he valued above all else, the lack of which he had identified as Vaughan Williams's biggest downfall: in a 1941 essay on 'England and the Folk-Art Problem' he admitted that 'Elgar represents the professional point of view, which emphasizes the importance of technical efficiency and welcomes any foreign influences that can be profitably assimilated' (*BoM* 31).

Britten's views could be equivocal, and they sometimes changed over time. Two composers whose music he drastically reconsidered were Brahms and Sibelius. Despite coming second or third in his pantheon in 1928, and despite Britten's framing a picture of him early in 1931,[27] Brahms had been unceremoniously dumped by 1934, his music now seeming 'solid, dull' (*JB* 218). Britten's view of Sibelius made the opposite transition. In 1963 he declared him as one of his favourites and provided a fulsome tribute in his centenary year of 1965,[28] but, in October 1946, putting down his thoughts on the first performance of his friend Jack Moeran's Symphony in G minor he cautioned that 'it has some excellent things in it, but terribly under the Sibelius influence – mood, ideas & technique. ItThis is going to be almost as bad as the Brahms influence on English music I fear' (379).

He was no less certain about what he wanted to hear in performance, often (if not invariably) praising Toscanini, for example, as well as Bridge (unsurprisingly). What he didn't want to hear was any performance under Boult. Britten's views of him in the early 1930s are unwaveringly consistent: 'I dislike Boult' (*JB* 56); '<u>terrible execrable</u> conductor' (87); 'to Queen's Hall to hear A. Boult sterilize Purcell's very lovely King Arthur … Boult at his worst & most typical' (290). In 1937 Boult conducted a performance of Britten's symphonic cycle *Our Hunting Fathers*. The composer admitted that he was 'marvellously painstaking', but nevertheless thought that 'he doesn't

---

[26] See the inter-chapter 'Performing'.
[27] See *JB* 14, 63.
[28] See *BoM* 248, 276–9.

really grasp the work' (428). He was equally scathing about the other major conducting force in London at that time, Henry Wood (1869–1944), with such comments as: 'H.J. Wood's usual eccentricies & meaningless vandalism' (127); 'Henry Wood conducting slack & incompetant perfs of Haydn Drum Symp.' (135); and 'Henry J. Wood is a public menace – and ought to be shot quickly, before he does much more murdering of classics ancient & modern' (274). There is one positive comment, distinctly at odds with the rest: 'Wood is really a marvel considering the amount he has to do' (373).

A note on influence

How do all these responses to his musical environment feed into Britten's own music, his intuitions about the nature of his own voice, and his conscious decisions about technical matters?

Spotting influences is a favourite pastime of concert-goers and professional musicians alike; one might question, though, whether it inevitably leads to greater musical understanding. Britten's indebtedness to other composers is mostly obvious. Pointing to the Mahlerian quality of the long melodic lines in the final parts of the Variations on a Theme of Frank Bridge and in his Sinfonia da Requiem is not an act of stunning critical insight; neither is the suggestion that the use of the saxophone in the Sinfonia is likely to have been prompted by the elegiac role of that instrument in Berg's Violin Concerto. Britten's appropriation of a Far Eastern sound-world in certain works from the late 1950s onwards is also straightforward to spot; since this often has a symbolic function, the music would be failing if the influence were not obvious. Less obvious, because it involves a technique or process rather than sound as such, is the derivation of Britten's intensive motivic working in Opp. 1, 2 and 3 from Schoenberg (but there is nothing that actually sounds like Schoenberg in Britten's output).

In all these cases and more, the simple logging of a source provides a little added perspective, but hardly leads to greater engagement on the part of the listener. What is important is how Britten's sources are bent to his purposes. At the extremes they may act as a catalyst and leave little or no trace; or they may provoke a reaction that, because it is so different from the source, is very hard to detect (in other words, the composer may write a work that functions at some level as a radical critique of the source). This makes the discussion of influence highly speculative; however, it doesn't mean that we can't learn something from our speculations, just so long as we recognize them as such.

Can we be precise about the formative role of the composers who are usually said to have had the most sustained influence on Britten – Berg, Stravinsky and Mahler? The structural and other parallels between Berg's Wozzeck and Britten's own first opera, Peter Grimes (1945), have often been noted, and Britten himself commented in 1966 that '"Wozzeck" had, for about ten years, played a great part in my life, not only, I may say musically, but also psychologically and emotionally ... I am aware now that I was strongly influenced by "Wozzeck" when I wrote "Grimes"' (*BoM* 292–3). But one wonders if there is any deeply embedded influence beyond this one work. Given Britten's equivocal view of the *Lyric Suite*, one might ask what, exactly, he might have got from the lessons with Berg that he hankered after during his later years at the RCM. He seems by then to have decided to move away from the totally chromatic world that Berg inhabited (infused with tonal references though it might have been). The two composers' expressive worlds are very different, and Berg's compulsion on occasion towards overwriting (the accumulation of detail swamping the ear) goes against Britten's impulse to strip down to the essentials. Perhaps the appeal was simply the quality of Berg's ideas, or the communicability of the music – or the sense of 'the new' arising from engagement with tradition. Possibly he was attracted by Berg's particular mixture of the strict and the free. As even a relatively cursory examination of the score of, say, *Wozzeck* shows, Berg was a constructivist, employing tightly worked schemes to control form, harmony and aspects of line – a framework within which, nonetheless, there was considerable opportunity for the improvisation of detail. From the little (very little!) that Britten has said about the actual business of composing, it seems that, while certainly not a constructivist in Berg's sense, he worked out broad schemes in advance, with the final part of the process being the 'finding' of the actual notes:

> The work is planned, and then when the plan of the work is fixed – is finished – the actual notes are decided on. (*BoM* 181)

> I never start a work without having a very clear conception of what that work is going to be. When I say conception, I don't mean necessarily tunes or specific rhythms or harmonies – or old-fashioned things like that! – but I mean the actual shape of the music – the kind of music it's going to be rather than the actual notes, they come very much later. But notes at this stage, which is about two or three weeks away from the first note to be put on paper – the notes are beginning to come already. Not necessarily the beginning, but little schemes throughout the work. I am beginning to plan it all from a textural point of view throughout. But there is always this element of chance, of improvisation, which happens once the work is under way. (323–4)

Regarding Stravinsky, Britten was attracted not so much to the works known for establishing his credentials as the pacemaker of musical modernism, but to the so-called neo-classical works (which were viewed by many as retrogressive). Despite his particular enthusiasm for the *Symphony of Psalms*, perhaps the more significant encounter was with *Apollon Musagète*, which Britten seems first to have heard in January 1931, in the same concert as the 'bewildering & terrifying' *Rite* (*JB* 62). That he doesn't mention *Apollo* (as the work is usually called) in his diary at the time does not mean that hearing it didn't have consequences – and the work's long stretches of diatonicism might well have reinforced Britten's decision at around the time he first heard the work to veer away from total chromaticism and reimagine the potential of the diatonic. Mahler might have been most significant for Britten in this latter regard, too. Mahler hardly shirks chromaticism, but the works Britten particularly enthuses about in his letters and diaries – the Fourth and Ninth Symphonies and the orchestral song-cycle *Kindertotenlieder* – all contain key passages of heightened diatonic expressivity. Later on in life (1963) Britten mentions being impressed with Mahler's 'sense of form; perhaps this is apparent from the [War] Requiem and the Spring Symphony' (*BoM* 244). However, Britten's forms tend to be much more compact, with little in the way of the vast parentheses and digressions for which Mahler is celebrated (or notorious, according to taste).

It is even more difficult to demonstrate 'negative influence' – influence as a critical response to composers Britten didn't like. In some ways it is odd that he so disliked Brahms, who was 'heavy-handed' (*BoM* 31) and who composed 'applied music – dull, ugly, gauch' (*JB* 393), for there are several aspects of approach that are similar. Brahms's music, too, is highly structured, and often sustained by the kinds of tonal and structural ambiguity that Britten employs, however differently elaborated. If Brahms's music sometimes seems over-determined, too schematic, lacking in spontaneity, this is something that has been levelled against Britten as well. And Britten's strong dislike of Vaughan Williams's music is no reason, either, not to note similarities and parallels – though whether these are genuinely the result of actual influence is (to stress the point again) impossible to say with certainty. With both composers there is a common investment in diatonicism as well as in certain modal usages.

London (cont.)

What we have observed thus far about Britten's life in London was entirely external to the reason for him being there – to study at the RCM. This accords with Britten's own view that his education 'was perhaps more outside the College than in it' (*BoM* 357). Although his official teacher for composition was John Ireland (1879–1962), Britten said that he 'saw Frank Bridge almost daily and I showed him every "major" work'. However, the diaries suggest that, while he had problems with Ireland (and not only musical ones – Carpenter indicates there are sources suggesting Ireland made a sexual pass at him), he did gain something from the relationship.

The problems revolved around Ireland not turning up to or being late for Britten's lessons, beginning in his very first week.[29] This was still

---

[29] *JB* 54.

happening in the month before he left the RCM, November 1933, and the situation was bad enough for Bridge to write a letter at the beginning of that year complaining about Britten's treatment.[30] At about this time Britten writes in his diary: 'There is some doubt as to whether I shall continue with Ireland at R.C.M.' (*JB* 127). Yet he also refers to having 'topping' and 'very good & instructive' lessons with him (55, 74), and later in life he recalled that Ireland, and his piano teacher Arthur Benjamin, were 'very kind' to him and 'really nurtured me very gently through a very, very difficult musical adolescence which I was going through at that time' (*BoM* 148). In 1959 he arranged an eightieth-birthday concert for Ireland, describing him in the programme note as 'a composer of strong personal gifts and real single-mindedness of purpose' (401–2). It was obviously not a smooth relationship at the time, though, and it is difficult to see what a composer as advanced as Britten was when he entered the RCM might have gained from the pastiche Palestrina exercises Ireland set him. As with Walton, but to a greater degree, it must have been clear to Ireland that Britten's facility and potential far outstripped his own.

It can be argued that students in higher education establishments learn as much, if not more, from their peers as from their teachers. There's little evidence that this was Britten's experience, though, and his fellow students feature remarkably few times in his diary. On the compositional side he seems to have had useful discussions with Grace Williams (1906–77), who was one of Vaughan Williams's students, but 'The attitude of most of the R.C.M. students was amateurish and folksy. That made me feel highly intolerant' (*BoM* 171). On the performance side, as well as having piano lessons from Arthur Benjamin, he formed a regular piano trio with Remo Lauricella (violin) and Bernard Richards (cello). Again, most of the performances in which he took part (and which he notes in his diary) were external to the RCM. This might be because he found the standards intolerably low, but it also suggests a lack of willingness to engage with what the institution had to offer. He also experienced difficulties in securing performances of his own work. When a performance of the Sinfonietta was finally scheduled, rehearsals were woefully lacking in commitment and professionalism: 'to R.C.M. in morning for the most atrocious of all rehearsals of my Sinfonietta. Only 8 inst. out of the 10 (& of these 3 new!)' (*JB* 117). The next day he and Ireland 'go & see Mr. Waddington & new arrangements are made that my Sinf. should sound less like ~~an anaem~~ aenemic cats'. Not that these arrangements had the required effect, for four weeks later he was complaining: 'Back to old style of rehearsal, only 8 people & 2 new!!' (121). The work did eventually receive an RCM performance, but the premiere was given externally by professionals at a Macnaghten-Lemare Concert.

---

[30] See *LL1* 146–7.

Though Britten's musical activities were almost all-consuming during his college years, he did find some time to explore the other arts. Some of his 'discoveries' had far-reaching, and extraordinary, consequences many years later. In June 1932, for instance, he listened to 'a wonderful, impressive but terribly eerie & scary play "The Turn of the Screw" by Henry James' (*JB* 106), which impressed him to the extent that he was reading it six months later; in the 1950s he worked it into one of his best-known operas.

'Down to real work'

Asked during one of the many interviews he agreed to during the late 1950s and 60s if he was 'glad to see the end of [his] student days', Britten replied, 'I only started enjoying myself as a human being after I left college and got down to real work' (*BoM* 172). His diaries suggest that this was not entirely the case. Britten's humour could be tinged with heavily sardonic flashes, and this response is likely to be just such an example. In any case, once he 'got down to real work' he did not always find it particularly enjoyable. In September 1936, three years after he left the RCM, he complained that 'My brain is getting completely fogged with so many activities' and then listed seven tasks. 'It's just a bit too much – but my fault for never saying "no" to anyone' (*JB* 372). And inevitably there were strains and stresses in his working relationships.

Saying 'no' is a risky option for a young musician trying to earn a living and build a reputation, and Britten seized every opportunity that came his way or which he managed to engineer. His professional career had kicked off with performances of his Opp. 1 and 2 in 1933 while he was still at the RCM and these works were also broadcast by the BBC in September and August respectively of that year. The Three Two-Part Songs had been accepted for publication by Oxford University Press (OUP), and in June and July 1933 he was negotiating the publication of *A Boy was Born*.[31] The latter drew positive notices, including a preview of the first performance by the composer Edmund Rubbra (1901–86), who saw in the work 'another sign of the growing vitality of modern English music': there was 'no trace of fumbling, nor, which is even more remarkable, of outside influences. His statements are always direct and to the point, and his musical language is easily understandable.'[32] The BBC broadcast was itself the result of a positive memo from the producer Victor Hely-Hutchinson, which concluded: 'I do whole-heartedly subscribe to the general opinion that Mr. Britten is the most interesting new arrival since Walton, and I

---

[31] See *SB* 17.
[32] Quoted in *BB* 53. Rubbra was not himself a composer Britten admired. His Piano Concerto was 'mild, unoriginal, ill constructed inefficient music' (March 1933, *JB* 135), while of his Symphony No. 1 Britten wrote in April 1937, 'I don't like this kind of music – infact I disapprove of it – but it is very well done of it's sort' (428).

feel that we should watch his work very carefully.'[33] The two institutions – OUP and the BBC – were important in launching and, in the case of the BBC, sustaining his career. By the time of Britten's departure for North America in 1939 the BBC had broadcast all his existing works with opus numbers – apart from *Ballad of Heroes*, Op. 14 (1939) – and most of them in their first performance.[34]

Britten's relationship with OUP broke down during 1933–4 – partly over their refusal to join the Performing Right Society – and in January 1935 Britten went over to their rivals, Boosey & Hawkes (B&H). Another factor in the break-up was the view of Hubert Foss, head of music publishing at OUP, that Britten was not writing sufficiently commercial works. An internal OUP memo written when B&H were expressing interest in publishing Opp. 1 and 2 states: 'it may be worth while to let Boosey waste some money on him so long as we can keep his more remunerative efforts.'[35] While Britten was already demonstrating his desire to provide 'useful' (and usually as a consequence 'more remunerative') music through works such as the *Simple Symphony* (well within the range of amateur string orchestras, and published by OUP in 1935) and a set of school songs, *Friday Afternoons* (which ended up with B&H, who published them in 1936), he was always going to want to realize greater musical ambitions. He therefore needed a publisher who would be prepared to invest in him in the long term. This was clearly seen as a risk: B&H's Directors sustained doubts about Britten's viability until the success of *Peter Grimes* in 1945.[36]

It was Ralph Hawkes, director of the London branch of B&H, who facilitated Britten's entrance into the world of music for film, theatre and the BBC.[37] This widened Britten's circle of contacts – literary (his collaborators included W. H. Auden and Christopher Isherwood) and musical – and the environment allowed him to try out effects without being in the spotlight. The requirement upon him to provide musical correlates for graphic or literary images was clearly useful as preparation for the composing of opera. However, Britten could be dismissive of film music, observing that 'It is usually impossible to underestimate the musical intelligence of the film audiences – certainly commercial ones'(*BoM* 28); and of the process of composing it he wrote, in connection with the famous GPO documentary, *Night Mail*, 'one cannot write "music" to these minute instructions, when even the speed of the beat and number

---

[33] Reproduced in *SB* 19.
[34] Britten's relationship with the BBC is explored in detail in Chapter 2 of *SB*.
[35] Helen Wallace, *Boosey & Hawkes: The Publishing Story* (London: Boosey & Hawkes, 2007), 12. See also Paul Kildea's highly detailed but lucid account of Britten's negotiations with OUP and his shift to B&H in *SB* 27–31.
[36] See the editorial note in *LL*1 339.
[37] Wallace, *Boosey & Hawkes*, 12.

of bars is fixed.'[38] And yet no critical commentary should downplay its role in helping him to develop and refine his professional skills.

One work that the BBC was relatively slow in broadcasting (seven months after its LPO premiere, in fact) was *Our Hunting Fathers*, Op. 8, completed in July 1936 and first performed at the Norwich Triennial Festival of that year. Announced by Britten as being his 'op. 1 alright' (*JB* 428), this was his first concert-hall collaboration with Auden (who selected the texts and wrote a prologue and epilogue), and is the work during this early period in which Britten gave his compositional ambitions the fullest rein. As with *A Boy was Born*, this is partly to do with length, but more notably to do with the performing forces (it was Britten's first professional full orchestral score and contains some ambitious effects) and with style and technique: there is more of an 'edge' to both sound and expression than in his previous scores, perhaps as a result of exploring parody in his film and theatre scores and in his Suite for violin and piano, Op. 6 (completed in June 1935, it was first performed at the 1936 International Society for Contemporary Music (ISCM) Festival in Barcelona in which Berg's Violin Concerto received its premiere).

The greater edge to sound and expression in *Our Hunting Fathers* is particularly apparent in the savagery of the 'Dance of Death', the fourth of the five movements, though irony and satire are rarely absent throughout. In technical terms the work is, like *A Boy was Born*, a tour-de-force of motivic manipulation. The main melodic source is a five-note 'package' that incorporates a conflict of mode, shifting from major to minor (though this is sometimes reversed). This shift has a history going back at least to Schubert and has powerful emotional connotations – of sadness, loss, threat, the workings of fate, and so on; and, in reverse, sudden optimism (though the shift to the major can also be used ironically). Used to powerful effect by Mahler in a number of works including the Sixth Symphony and *Kindertotenlieder*, it continued to be a resource for Britten throughout his career.

While the ostensible subject-matter of *Our Hunting Fathers* is humankind's treatment of animals, its relationship with contemporary politics has long been recognized. Britten's diaries, no doubt reflecting discussions in the left-wing-dominated environment of the film and theatre groups for which he worked, are scattered with political comments. As Donald Mitchell was the first to point out, *Our Hunting Fathers* makes a couple of allusions to the gathering Nazi menace: 'given the situation at home and abroad in 1936, and the prevailing conviction among so many intellectuals that Europe and European culture were done for, a prayer to rid the world of a plague of rats [in the second movement, 'Rats Away!'] must have seemed strikingly

---

[38] Donald Mitchell, *Britten and Auden in the Thirties* (London: Faber & Faber, 1981), 81.

appropriate',[39] and Mitchell comments that since the deadpan juxtaposition of the words 'German' and 'Jew' (in the roll-call of dogs' names in the 'Dance of Death') does not occur in the original Ravenscroft poem it can be taken as a deliberate 'intervention'. Both allusions could easily be missed; what the first audience would not have missed was the in-your-face condemnation of the hunting that for many of them would have been a perfectly acceptable pastime.

Our Hunting Fathers is a rare example of Britten offering music that paid little regard to the experience and expectations of its first audience (provincial and 'county'), and which elicited grumbles from the performers. Reviewers noted what they regarded as the obscurity of Auden's text, and general 'difficulty'.[40] Faced with original effects and high technical demands, the orchestra misbehaved. Vaughan Williams, whose *Five Tudor Portraits* was premiered in the same concert, lectured them between rehearsals about the need for professional standards,[41] after which things improved a little.

It was not the first time that Britten had received a negative response from critics, and it wouldn't be the last; but if the vagaries of critical opinion simply had to be borne, connecting with his audience and having players on his side was of the utmost importance. After the initial broadcast, *Our Hunting Fathers* largely disappeared from sight until a couple of recordings were issued after the composer's death. When Peter Pears sang it for the first time in 1950 it was the work's second concert performance, and Britten seems to have revived it only once thereafter, for a BBC broadcast in 1961. Perhaps it is not incidental that the ensuing larger works, the Variations on a Theme of Frank Bridge, Op. 10 (1937) and the Piano Concerto, Op. 13 (1938), move away from harder-edged, modernist-sounding textures and draw more on 'characteristic' types – ready-made points of engagement for the audience that can be manipulated to create whatever effect is sought. It is difficult not to believe that there was a commercial aspect to this, encouraged by his publishers.[42] That Britten was very conscious of how he was being judged is apparent from his sardonic diary entry about the first performance of his second Auden-based work, the collection of songs entitled *On this Island*: 'They have a public success, but not a succès d'estime – they are far too obvious and amenable for Contempory music' (*JB* 461). In this the voice part is less virtuosic, the musical 'language' is more traditional (the harmony is more triadic), and the final number has a popular-song basis.

The Variations on a Theme of Frank Bridge was the work that announced Britten to a European audience. It was commissioned by Boyd Neel for his

[39] Ibid., 35.
[40] See *LL1* 448–9.
[41] *JB* 483, note 125.
[42] See Wallace, *Boosey & Hawkes* 13.

string orchestra, and received its first performance in The Netherlands before being played at the event for which it was actually commissioned, the 1937 Salzburg Festival. Britten was not present, but Pears (whom he had met about five months previously) was visiting the city on holiday and wrote an account of the occasion to the composer, describing the work's success.[43] The Variations were conceived by Britten as a tribute to his teacher (the theme comes from the second of Bridge's *Three Idylls* for string quartet), exploring his attributes as follows:[44]

Introduction and Theme	To F.B. – himself
Adagio	His integrity
March	His energy
Romance	His charm
Aria Italiana	His wit
Bourrée Classique	His tradition
Wiener Waltzer	His gaiety
Moto Perpetuo	His enthusiasm
Funeral March	His sympathy (understanding)
Chant	His reverence
Fugue	His skill
and	
Finale	Our affection

Clearly 'Our affection' was always going to command the emotional peak of the work, and, appropriately, it is the most personal movement; with the exception of the opening fanfare (which is a very public gesture) and the *Adagio*, the work consists of characteristic (or genre) pieces and parodies. But what is at least as interesting as the tribute aspect of the work (the Fugue includes quotations from a number of Bridge's works) is Britten's assertion of his own identity: it is his Oedipal moment, his own supremely confident musical athleticism blowing away Bridge's inward-looking, wistful lyricism.

Bridge himself wrote appreciatively of the dedication,[45] but there were some ructions over other works at around this time. Again it is a letter from Marjorie Fass, to her friend Daphne Oliver the day after the first performance of Britten's Piano Concerto, which shows the degree to which the circle (and presumably Bridge himself, too) could be disapproving: 'Dear Benjy doesn't know how deeply disappointed we all are, but he will one day. We

---

[43] Christopher Headington, *Peter Pears: A Biography* (London: Faber & Faber, 1992), 72–3.
[44] See LL1 502–3.
[45] LL1 503.

all adored the Dvorak [Eighth Symphony] after the Benjy work & all said the same thing of it – here is music – and in its degree beautifully made – what a relief.'[46] Philip Brett perhaps touches on the 'problem' they had with the piano concerto: 'After the responsible, serious instrumental pieces of the 1930s, this display of high spirits touched with sentimentality indicates a willingness to abandon a too-limiting decorum and give in to sensuality.'[47] The concerto commission was for the Proms, and as such was the biggest single platform Britten had yet had for his work (and for himself as performer, since he played the solo part), and there is no doubt that he was alive to the career-developing opportunities. It was his first engagement with a 'standard' large-scale genre, and – unlike *Our Hunting Fathers* – it was well-tailored for the occasion, fulfilling expectations concerning showmanship while maintaining interest with considerable harmonic and formal wit.

Struggles

The confident utterance of the major works mentioned thus far belies the insecurity that was the relentless companion of the composer for the whole of his life. If there was a solid core of certainty in his mind about his abilities and the direction in which he wanted to go, it was constantly assailed by a swirling fog of doubt. His diaries log his frustration with trying to get pieces right. Here, for example, is his entry for 25 January 1935: 'Still my writing won't go right. I have been trying off and on for about 18 months to finish a quartet suite [*Alla Quartetto serioso: 'Go play, boy, play'*], & I am still as stuck as ever-; I can't begin the extra mov. to the Vln suite; and I have the scheme but no notes yet for my St Cecelea Hymn' (*JB* 245). *Our Hunting Fathers* was no easier. On 5 June 1936: 'Spend morning & most of afternoon writing practically finishing Messalina – but spend rest of day thoroughly depressed not being able to decide whether the stuff is the best or worst stuff I've ever written. Most probably it's neither – that's the trouble!' (357). But it wasn't just his music that he was struggling with, and he confesses later in the same entry: 'Life is a pretty hefty struggle these days – sexually as well. Decisions are so hard to make, & its difficult to look unprejudised on apparently abnormal things' (358).

Britten's diary entry for the first day of 1936, in which he sums up his life's 'state of play', expresses an acute sense of inferiority when in the company of older, more experienced collaborators: 'having a bad inferiority complex in company of brains like Basil Wright, Wystan Auden & William Coldstream' (*JB* 323).[48] Given that the issue of his sexuality was looming

---

[46] *LL1* 577.
[47] *BBGO*.
[48] Wright and Coldstream were, along with Auden, some of Britten's colleagues in the GPO Film Unit.

large, the sexual confidence of the likes of Auden and Isherwood was probably quite intimidating too.

Britten's diaries are generally restrained when it comes to sexual matters:

> He [Piers Dunkerley] is a nice thing and I am very fond of him – thank heaven not sexually, but I am getting to such a condition that I am lost without some children (of either sex) near me. (15 April 1936, *JB* 346)

> After the concert [during the Barcelona ISCM Festival] go with L.B. [Lennox Berkeley], Peter Burra, & AC. to a night club in China town – my 1st & not particularly pleasant experience – as a young harlot is very keen on picking my pockets tho' I loose nothing. The dancing (mostly male – & dressed as females) is very lovely. But my god the sordidity – & the sexual temptations of every kind at each corner. (22 April 1936, 349)

> [After a conversation with his brother Robert:] In fact this time I have felt much more warmth towards him, in spite of his obstinate conservatism in so many ways. Actually on our evening walks we have had very intimate discussions & he hasn't been shocked by, but even helped with sympathy & advice, my 'queerness'. (4 April 1937, 422)

> [Lennox Berkeley] is a dear & I am very, very fond of him; nevertheless, it is a comfort that we can arrange sexual matters to at least <u>my</u> satisfaction. (11 April 1937, 423)

> [After a visit to a Jermyn St Turkish bath with Isherwood:] Very pleasant sensations – completely sensuous, but very healthy. It is extraordinary to find one's resistance to anything gradually weakening. The trouble was that we spent the night there – couldn't sleep a wink on the hard beds, in the perpetual restlessness of the surroundings. (3 July 1937, 440)

Some of these entries are more coded than others, but the general tone suggests uncertainty and inhibition. It can be argued that the guardedness should not be surprising because British society was cripplingly inhibited in general at that period. But Britten is writing this for his eyes only. Unless he was being very guarded indeed, his report of his visit to the Turkish bath with Isherwood on 3 July 1937 is also extraordinarily naive, with no awareness, apparently, that the whole point of the establishment was to provide a place for gay men to have sexual encounters (the expression 'very healthy' suggests that Britten's trying to convince himself that nothing 'sordid', such as he witnessed in Barcelona, was taking place). There seem to have been a number of people, including Auden and Isherwood, who were keen to help Britten acknowledge and act upon his sexual identity. Whether this was of any help to him is impossible to say, but one imagines that it was just as likely to increase his anxiety and unhappiness.

Is there any reflection of Britten's anxiety about sex in his music of this period? Carpenter's view that *On this Island* demonstrates that 'romantic and sexual non-fulfilment was a theme that currently held his attention' applies essentially to only one of the texts. And while one verse of 'Now the leaves are falling fast' –

> Whispering neighbours, left and right,
> Pluck us from the real delight;
> And the active hands must freeze
> Lonely on the separate knees.

– could certainly be interpreted as being about the oppression of gay love (even if it's hard to see how the accompaniment projects this as specifically gay, as Carpenter suggests[49]), it is difficult to make a case for other examples of the encoding of gay subjectivity.

The 'appalling ache & loneliness' Britten referred to on 18 February 1937 followed the death of his mother on 31 January. His father had died on 5 April 1934 while Britten was in Florence at the ISCM Festival, but on account of his particular closeness to his mother her death affected him deeply – not least because he had pressed her to come to London to nurse his sister Beth, from whom his mother probably caught the influenza that led to her demise (Imogen Holst, daughter of Gustav Holst, and later Britten's assistant, wrote in her diary that Britten had felt 'responsible for his mother's death & it had taken ages to realize that he hadn't been'[50]). Interestingly, over the following months the intensity of Britten's discussion with various people about sexual matters appears to increase (or at least is noted more frequently in his diary). Perhaps his mother's death eased the shackles a little. Basil Reeve thought so: 'Certainly when the mother died, there was a great sense of release. I mean, Ben's personal life started.'[51]

It was a mere five weeks after his mother died that Britten met Peter Pears. He is first mentioned in his diary, misspelt, on 6 March. The impression was not entirely positive – 'Lunch with T.H., Peter Piers, & Douglas – at their flat – with interesting tho' snobbish & superficial arguments' (*JB* 415); it is possible, though, that the snobbishness and superficiality came from the other parties and not Pears. It was a number of months before they became lovers; indeed, there is a question over the degree of commitment on Britten's side for some time. Their friendship blossomed quickly, though. The key event was a journey with Pears – first by train, then on Pears's motorbike with Britten riding pillion – to sort out Peter Burra's effects in a cottage Pears had shared with him.[52] Burra, who had died in a flying

---

[49] *BB* 105.
[50] *BB* 97.
[51] *BB* 97.
[52] *JB* 430. Pears himself said that this was his first 'real meeting with Ben': see Headington, *Peter Pears*, 67.

3. *Britten reading in a rural idyll, c. 1929.*

accident, was a close friend of Pears's, and they had been at Lancing School and Oxford together.

Various subsequent meetings between Britten and Pears are logged in Britten's diary – concerts, lunches, games of tennis, and, on 8 September 1937, an overnight stay at Britten's home during which they 'talk till a late hour' (*JB* 450). The next day they run through some of Britten's music (a song from his score for the BBC radio feature, *The Company of Heaven*, the first music he wrote specifically for Pears) and Britten declares Pears to be 'a good singer & a first-rate musician' (451). The next month Pears 'comes to lunch & to stay for the week here' (457). A few days after that Britten is noting that 'if he studies he will be a very good singer ... He's certainly one of the nicest people I know, but frightfully reticent' (457–8). The date on which they began to give recitals is not clear, but it is thought to have been in 1937.[53]

They moved into a London flat together in February 1938, but Britten was also spending a good deal of time in his new home in Suffolk, which was bought with money left to him by his mother. He and Pears clearly missed each other when apart, with exchanges of 'longing to see you' in their letters.

It is during the mid-1930s that we begin to witness the strong effect of the physical environment upon Britten – especially apparent during his stay at Crantock on the Cornish coast while composing *Our Hunting Fathers* in 1936. During this visit he went for long walks despite the bad weather, and one such walk elicits one of the most moving entries in his diary:

> After a dull & wet early morning the weather at last clears & the evening is heavenly. I am terribly worried (& injured – so hermit-minded have I become!) by new arrivals in neighbouring huts. Too many signs of life – and a gramophone. Too much like civilisation. I eventually go out for a terrific walk along cliffs well past Holywell – starting at 11.0 don't arrive back till 3.30. I have never enjoyed a walk so much – and the climax is when I find a colossal chasm in the rocks – miles away from civilisation – climb an enormous distance down to rocky shore & undress & bathe stark naked. The sheer sensual exstasy of it! – ~~cop~~ coupled with the real danger (currents & submerged rocks) & doubts whether I shall be able to climb the tortuous path to the top. Utter bliss. (*JB* 363)

Contemplating another part of the country, the Cotswolds, about a year later, he decided that his home county was unsurpassed: 'Walk with Beth over glorious hills in morning ... I love this country – but actually not with the same affection as Suffolk. I always feel that Suffolk is the genuine article, while this is aspiring to something that is outside its compass'

[53] Headington, *Peter Pears*, 75.

(*JB* 432). A few weeks after writing this he was actively looking for somewhere in Suffolk to live, and settled on the Old Mill at Snape, which he renovated to his own specifications. He moved in on 9 April 1938, and found his new situation idyllic: 'The country is heavenly & the view from the Mill superb' (468). Britten's recognition of the importance to him of the locale of his birth was later to acquire enormous significance, while the notion of the idyllic, transformed in various ways (and normally glimpsed but not attained), underpins much, perhaps the majority, of his most powerful work.

But he was not entirely settled: a little more than a year later he was making plans to leave for the United States.

Boys

From the mid-1950s, if not earlier, Britten's interest in boys was as much an open secret as his relationship with Pears. During rehearsals for his setting of *Noye's Fludde*, Op. 59 (1957), which is dedicated 'To my nephew and nieces, Sebastian, Sally and Roguey Welford, and my young friend Roger Duncan' and was composed for children's forces led by a handful of adult professionals, the conductor, Charles Mackerras, made a comment that was to threaten his continuing involvement with the Aldeburgh Festival. Bridcut relates the story in his ground-breaking book, *Britten's Children*, which draws on the interviews he made for his 2004 film of the same name:

> In the final stages of rehearsal for the first performance in June 1958, the children were ferried by coach to and from halls in Aldeburgh and Thorpeness, and eventually to the parish church in Orford. It meant that Aldeburgh and its environs were visibly flooded with young boys and girls, and several of the adult musicians started to snigger about the number of boys surrounding Britten. 'Some of us mocked the idea', Mackerras recalls, 'and we said, "Well, now this is Ben's paradise!" We were rather derisive about the whole thing.'[1]

Mackerras's comment found its way to Britten, who promptly sent for him, made it clear how upset he was by the remark, and asked: 'Am I a lecher just because I enjoy the company of children?'[2] Mackerras stated to Bridcut that he didn't believe 'it had ever occurred to [Britten] that we found any of this amusing or unusual'. Whether or not sexual attraction to boys was regarded simply as 'amusing' in the 1950s, it is certainly not thought of in that way in the twenty-first century, and is a subject likely to bring a good deal of discomfort to admirers of Britten's music and other aspects of his personal conduct.

The last-named dedicatee of *Noye's Fludde*, Roger Duncan, the son of Britten's friend Ronald Duncan, is one of the boys befriended by Britten who was interviewed by Bridcut. Duncan admitted to Bridcut that Britten had a sexual interest in him, but that the feelings were not reciprocated:

---

[1] BC 236.
[2] BC 237.

'I admired him and enjoyed being with him. I enjoyed and liked his affection, his care, and the attention he gave me. But I wasn't attracted to him physically.'

'But perhaps he was to you?' [Bridcut] ventured.

'Oh I'm sure. That was quite plain. But he respected the fact that I was not.'[3]

When Duncan went to Harrow and was teased about his relationship with Britten, he discussed the matter with the composer, who fully accepted that Duncan wasn't homosexual. 'He used to kiss me, and that was about all.'[4] Commenting on the details of such recollections may seem doubly discomforting, but it should perhaps be pointed out that Duncan was in fact aged 11 when their friendship began, so that, even if Britten's sexual attraction manifested itself two or three years later, it would seem to be paedophiliac in nature rather than homosexual; and the fact that it was Britten who did the kissing points to what seems to be an abuse of a power relationship, all the more so when one considers that Britten had brokered a bizarre quasi-adoption of Duncan with his father.[5]

Another boy befriended by Britten, Jonathan Gathorne-Hardy, told Bridcut about his having anticipated an advance and warding it off. This was when he was with Britten at Crag House in Aldeburgh, the composer's home from 1947. As Bridcut relates: 'they had each had a bath after playing tennis, and were standing in their towels. Ben put his arms around him – a moment Jonny had anticipated, because he remembers announcing somewhat operatically, "No, Ben, it is not to be". Gathorne-Hardy says he never felt threatened by Britten, who behaved with gentleness and delicacy.'[6]

This incident occurred when Gathorne-Hardy was 18, but he first met Britten when he was 14 and was 'at once aware I attracted him'. It is clear from Bridcut's interviews, though, that many of Britten's 'boy companions', as Bridcut calls them, were unaware of any sexual interest from him, even if associated adults had concerns – as in the case of Humphrey Maud, whose father, Sir John Maud, Permanent Secretary at the Ministry of Education, called Britten to his office and forbade his son further holidays at Britten's house.[7] Humphrey himself later stated that 'it was a

---

[3] BC 224.
[4] BC 226.
[5] See LL4 269–70, which reproduces Ronald Duncan's account in Ronald Duncan, *Working with Britten: A Personal Memoir* (Welcombe: The Rebel Press, 1981).
[6] BC 160.
[7] BC 151.

very intimate, no-holds-barred, relationship. But there was absolutely no physical implication or connotation whatsoever in this.'[8] Indeed, all of the boys interviewed – including David Hemmings, later a renowned actor, who created the part of Miles in *The Turn of the Screw*, during which Britten became particularly close to him – insist that there was a complete absence of what David Spenser, Harry in the first production of *Albert Herring*, refers to as 'hanky-panky',[9] and attest to Britten's kindness and ability to engage with them on their level. The composer Robert Saxton, who met and corresponded with him during the 1960s, described him as being someone of 'great safety, comforting and very polite'.[10]

The one case with strong suggestions of a sexual approach from Britten is that of Harry Morris, who died in 2002 and was therefore not interviewed by Bridcut, though his wife was. Morris was a 13-year-old boy from a working-class home, whose mother became known to Britten's sister Barbara through her Women's Voluntary Service work (Britten refers to Morris in his diary for 3 July 1936 as 'the little boy Barbara found … He is getting on with his fiddle, & sings very nicely, & seems very intelligent' (*JB* 361)). Bridcut explains that Britten 'was determined to do his bit by raising the boy's sights and giving him opportunities that his family could not contemplate'.[11]

As part of the project Britten invited him to the family holiday in Crantock in 1937, the year after his idyllic summer there composing *Our Hunting Fathers*. This stay was far from idyllic, however: the holiday was riven with tension between Britten and his brother Robert (erupting in a quick trip to London that they undertook together in the middle of it), and Harry Morris did not stay as long as planned. Bridcut describes what he could discover about the events thus:

> Whether the boy felt uncomfortable in this family stand-off, or whether it had always been planned that way, Harry Morris left Cornwall early. He himself always maintained it was a sudden departure, for a quite different reason. In later life he told his wife Beryl and their son Tim that he had been alarmed by what he understood as a sexual approach from Britten in his bedroom. He said he screamed, and hit Britten with a chair. This brought Beth rushing into the room, who, he said, shouted at her brother. She and Ben

---

[8] BC 150.
[9] BC 156.
[10] BC 5.
[11] BC 46.

37

left, and Beth locked the door. Harry got dressed, packed his bags, and sat waiting for the morning. Without speaking, Beth took him to the station, and dispatched him to London. When he reached home, he told his mother what had happened, but she told him off and refused to believe his story. He never told his father.[12]

No mention is made in Britten's diary of Morris's departure. There is some contact with Morris in London in October and then February 1938, but none thereafter. It is of course impossible to know exactly what happened, but the fact that, in old age, a visit to Crantock made Morris ill[13] suggests that his experience of 1937 was profoundly unsettling for him.

If there is no evidence that this overstepping of boundaries, if that is indeed what this was, happened again, Britten was to continue to find himself infatuated, and this had a significant effect in shaping aspects of his life. For example, one of the motivations for his departure for North America may have been to escape the turmoil of his infatuation with Wulff Scherchen, the son of the conductor Hermann Scherchen; Britten first met Wulff when the boy was 13, during his visit to Barcelona in 1936. It was two years later that they began to spend a good deal of time together, Scherchen frequently staying with Britten in his new home in the Old Mill, Snape. Their correspondence suggests an emotional involvement of escalating intensity with expressions of love on both sides (and much poetry on Scherchen's).

Scherchen seems to have proved a more congenial object of affection than Lennox Berkeley, whose attentions Britten rebuffed.[14] Berkeley wrote to Britten in late 1938 or early 1939 that it was 'almost impossible for me not to be haunted by the green-eyed monster when Wulff is with you'.[15] Britten was by then sharing a flat with Pears when he needed to be in London. Pears saw the consummation of his and Britten's relationship as taking place just after they entered the United States in 1939, but Britten's correspondence shows that he continued to yearn for Scherchen until around the middle of 1942, up to which point he served as something of a muse.

Britten's major infatuation during his time in the United States seems, however, to have been with Bobby Rothman, the son of David Rothman, who owned a music and hardware store on Long Island. They spent relatively little time together, and the

---

[12] *BC* 51–2.
[13] *BC* 46.
[14] *JB* 500.
[15] *BC* 74.

passion was not reciprocal – as Bridcut says, 'Bobby points out that he saw Ben for no more than ten days in total across a three-year period, and he was completely unaware that Britten had any sort of crush on him.'[16] Evidence of Britten's infatuation is scarce, with nothing beyond Britten's writing to Rothman that he had 'a large photo of you staring at me all the time when I'm working'[17] and his admitting to Beata Mayer (the daughter of the household that Britten and Pears were then staying with) that, as Carpenter says, 'he had fallen in love with young Bobby Rothman'.[18] This infatuation, nevertheless, may well lie behind what Britten later described as the 'mental perplexities' he was suffering from at the time.

Did Britten see his sexual attraction to boys as separate, or separable, from his obvious affinity for the childish mind? He responded to an appreciative comment by Imogen Holst on the setting of the boys' song in Act III scene 2 of *Gloriana* ('Now rouse up all the city') by saying, 'it's because I'm still 13,'[19] and aspects of his behaviour – his keeping, at the age of 40, a schoolboy diary in which he faithfully recorded his weight, height, bicycle number, and so on;[20] his attempt to walk across a carpet without stepping on the lines of the pattern in order to find out whether or not he was a good composer;[21] and his liking for nursery food – might encourage us to take this literally. Perhaps his close friendship with a series of boys resulted in large part simply from his enjoyment in spending as much time as possible in that world.

Boyhood in its most straightforward, unencumbered sense is certainly celebrated in his music – in the boys' choir sections of the *Spring Symphony*, Op. 44 (1949), for example, and in the songs he wrote for his brother's school, *Friday Afternoons*, Op. 7 (1934). Celebrations of adult–child relationships are not to be found, however. Those of his works that have a boy as a central character – *The Turn of the Screw*, Op. 54 (1954) and *Death in Venice*, Op. 88 (1973) – revolve around the consequences of an adult male being sexually attracted to the boy (implicitly in the former, explicitly in the latter), and in each case there are tragic consequences. Yet if *The Turn of the Screw* is, on at least one level, a warning of the waste and destruction that results when the greatest sexual taboo

[16] *BC* 119.
[17] *BC* 120.
[18] *BB* 161.
[19] Christopher Grogan (ed.), *Imogen Holst: A Life in Music* (Woodbridge: Boydell Press, 2007), 199.
[20] *BC* 2.
[21] Duncan, *Working with Britten*, 86.

in modern Western society is swept aside, it seems extraordinary that Britten should risk disaster through people's perceptions of his liaison with David Hemmings while the first performance of the opera was being prepared. Is this breathtaking naivety, or did he see his attraction to Hemmings (and, by implication, the other boys) as something other – as being, in contrast with Quint's treatment of Miles, in some sense pure? But then Myfanwy Piper, the librettist for *The Turn of the Screw*, is quoted by Carpenter as saying about Britten's friendship with boys that 'He would go for long walks – I remember one occasion when he did, perhaps two – and he would say that it was very upsetting for him, worrying. He found it a temptation, and he was very worried about it.'[22] Further complicating matters is the possibility that, as Carpenter puts it, some of the boys may 'to some extent have made the advance themselves': Donald Mitchell recalled Britten saying to him, 'It's often a problem that these youngsters seem to think I want to go to bed with them.'[23] Basil Douglas, the general manager of the English Opera Group during the 1940s and 50s, suggested to Bridcut that Hemmings, 'just like Tadzio [the boy in *Death in Venice*], enjoyed his hold over the older man'.[24]

Britten's relationship with boys is likely to remain an uncomfortable issue, and if there are ultimately unanswerable questions, that is not to say that they should be put to one side. Early in his book Bridcut writes that

> Britten assumed an openness and transparency in his dealings with boys that prevented any secret desire devouring him through repression and denial. It was a sublimation which enabled him to control his weakness – perhaps even to transform it into something wholesome and good, as it emerged in his friendships and his music. This is why he always needed to have a favourite of the moment: it was an essential part of his creativity, and of his knowledge and understanding of himself.[25]

This is perhaps taking a little too much on trust: even if some of the boys interviewed were aware of the full range of Britten's feelings for them, it must be questioned whether they could fully understand them, and know how to deal with them. Artistic sublimation transforming his 'weakness ... into something wholesome and good' could not, however remarkable the music,

---

[22] BB 354.
[23] Ibid.
[24] BC 198.
[25] BC 6.

mitigate any emotional scarring of individual boys. While we cannot conclude – without the properly constituted testing of evidence – that Britten's actions were responsible for Harry Morris's distress (in other words, condemning him as a lecher, and more), equally, we are in no position to dismiss Morris's account.

TWO

GOING WEST (1939–1942)

I'm thinking hard about the future. This <u>may</u> be the Country. There's
so much that is unknown about it – & it is tremendously large &
beautiful. <u>And</u> it is enterprising and vital. (*LL2* 668, to Wulff
Scherchen)

I am <u>certain</u> that N. America is the place of the future. (671, to Beth)

Everyday America's destroyed and re-created,
America is what you do,
America is I and you,
America is what you choose to make it.

The third quotation is from a speech given by the eponymous hero
towards the end of Britten and Auden's operetta *Paul Bunyan*, which was
completed in New York in April 1941, two years after Britten and Pears
followed Auden and Isherwood to North America, and landed at Quebec,
Canada in May 1939. Bunyan was the mythic lumberjack who cleared
American forests and made way for civilization; he could be said to be the
epitome of the American 'can-do' attitude.

In some ways *Paul Bunyan* is the most important of Britten's American
works, even though it was subsequently withdrawn and not performed
again until the final years of his life, and even though (as the withdrawal
suggests) it was far from being the most polished or accomplished music
from that period. Although not a full-length opera, it gave Britten vital
theatrical experience beyond the incidental music that he had composed
in London. It enabled him to develop aspects of characterization,
symbology, and large-scale structure. It must also have clarified the
collaborative conditions under which he could work or, rather, couldn't –
for working with Auden seems not to have been an entirely smooth
operation at all times.

The work ends with an upbeat, utopian statement, and yet stretches of
Paul Bunyan are quite critical of the American reality as Britten and Auden

saw it (this inevitably led to a hostile reception from some critics). Britten's acutely divided response to the United States is made clear in letters 'back home' in April 1940 to his brother-in-law Kit Welford (Beth's husband) and to Enid Slater (wife of Montagu Slater, who was to write the libretto of *Peter Grimes*). To Welford he sketches 'a rough idea of how this country strikes one' (*LL2* 793). On the one hand it 'seems to have the corruption of the Old World & little of its tradition or charm', possessing 'all the infuriating qualities of youth without any of its redeeming qualities'; and he is unequivocal that he hates New York. On the other, the US 'is <u>not</u> engaged solely with killing people (altho' she may be thinking of it more every day) – enterprise <u>still</u> is rewarded in this country, & I'm sure there is a future for this country altho' the next decade or so may be very black' (794). To Enid Slater he was out-and-out negative: 'I hate to have to admit it, but America seems to be letting us down in every way. I don't mean us personally, so much as all the things one believes in. She is so narrow, so self-satisfied, so chauvinistic, so superficial, so reactionary, & above all so <u>ugly</u>. People & Scenery' (800). Yet if there seems no reason to believe that *Paul Bunyan*'s two creators were naive enough to think that America would fulfil all their desires, there is no reason either to believe that, from their rather different perspectives, they thought it would provide anything other than significant opportunities.

For Britten, there seem to have been at least as many reasons to leave, even escape, the UK and go simply anywhere as there were positive reasons to go specifically to North America. But some uncertainty lingered over whether leaving home was an entirely good idea. During the transatlantic voyage Britten wrote to Wulff Scherchen: 'What a fool one is to come away – the more I think of Snape & the visits to Cambridge & yours to Snape – the more I feel a fool to have left it all.'[1] While the crisis in Britten's relationship with Wulff may have been a significant factor behind his leaving the UK, separation – initially at least – seems to have made him long for Wulff even more, delaying his complete commitment to Pears for some time. Britten implies that he was having a problematic relationship with someone in his letter to Copland announcing he was on his way to Canada: 'I got heavily tied up in a certain direction, which is partly why I'm crossing the ocean!' (*LL2* 634). While this is assumed by most commentators to refer to Wulff, he might equally have meant Lennox Berkeley. It seems that Britten hadn't, in fact, managed to resolve matters with Berkeley, and to Pears just over a month before they set off he wrote: 're. [Berkeley] we've had a bit of a crisis and I'm only too thankful to be going away' (*LL1* 616). Indeed, two sources – Jackie Hewett, Isherwood's boyfriend at the time, and John Evans's reminiscences of conversations he'd had with Pears after Britten's death –

---

[1] *BC* 90.

state that Britten and Berkeley were having a sexual relationship, and that (in Evans's words) 'Ben was happy to get out of it'.[2]

It is hardly surprising that the explanations for leaving that Britten and Pears later gave publicly make no reference to any of this – or to any feeling of alienation because of their sexual orientation. Their reasons revolve rather around disenchantment with the political situation and the difficulty they envisaged they'd have in the UK as pacifists and conscientious objectors should war in Europe break out, as seemed inevitable. In a 1959 interview in *High Fidelity Magazine* Britten insisted that he wasn't running away from war: 'But I wanted nothing to do with a military system that, to me, was part of Europe's decay. Mistakenly, as it turned out, I felt that Europe was finished. And it seemed to me that the New World was so much *newer*, so much readier to welcome new things' (*BoM* 173). He went on to say that Pears was going to America 'on holiday', which conflicts with all other accounts, including Pears's own:

> It was really in '38 that Ben began to feel that he wasn't doing much good, although he had actually done quite well … And in '39, Ben and I decided that he was not getting anywhere fast enough, as it were … He was dissatisfied, he wanted to get away from Europe and the approaching war. We were both pacifists, and we didn't see ourselves doing very much … Ben had an offer of a film in Hollywood and I decided that I'd go off with him to America.[3]

Britten tends as well to give the impression that the trip was well-planned and thought through, which was clearly not the case – it was much more a matter of having a rough initial itinerary, making a few arrangements with contacts that Pears had made during his US tour with the New English Singers in 1936, and seeing where this would lead them.

It certainly was not entirely accurate for Britten to feel that he wasn't doing very well, when he was receiving a good number of performances on BBC radio, including a full programme of his music the week before they left for America. It was true, though, that he was reliant on the BBC to a perhaps risky extent: they could decide at any moment (for whatever reason – their programming decisions were not accountable to any outside organization) that they no longer wished to give him so much air-time. This might explain a passage from a letter Britten wrote to Mary Behrend (an enthusiastic patron of the arts who later commissioned Britten's Second String Quartet) just before setting sail: 'the real reason [for going] is to do some really intensive thinking & for me personally to do somework to please <u>myself</u> & not necessarily the BBC or Basil Dean!' (*LL1* 618). In the 1959 *High Fidelity Magazine* interview he also mentioned a lack of opportunities:

---

[2] *BB* 127.
[3] Quoted from the 1985 Central Television documentary *The Tenor Man's Song*, in Christopher Headington, *Peter Pears: A Biography* (London: Faber & Faber, 1992), 83.

REID: ... I always had the impression that after leaving college you prospered rather.

BRITTEN: Not really. A day came when the G.P.O. Film Unit no longer wanted me. One had a struggle to get things performed.

REID: Which is why you decided to settle in America?

BRITTEN: Money was not really the issue. Frustration was more important. It was frustration that sent me to America. I felt there was a wall of laziness and apathy against new things. (*BoM* 172)

It seems that, initially, Britten and Pears were not entirely clear whether their relocation was going to be short- or long-term. Wulff Scherchen was under the impression that 'it was just a temporary measure. He was not emigrating'.[4] Meanwhile, in that same letter to Mary Behrend, Britten wrote: 'Peter'll be back at the end of the summer, but I have other ideas & may stay on abit or go to U.S.A.' (*LL1* 618). Once in America their plans began to change, however. Pears was unable to return as soon as he had originally envisaged because of the outbreak of war. And Britten had already begun at least to entertain a long-term stay: the second quotation at the head of this chapter, from a letter to Beth dated 25 June 1939, is preceded by the statement, 'I might as well confess it now, that I am seriously considering staying over here permanently.' Yet he is 'terribly torn' and his future is 'so much in the air' (*LL2* 671). Other letters of the time, too, were riven with uncertainty and quickly developing homesickness. To Beth, for example, he wrote: 'I feel <u>terribly</u> homesick, my dear. Yearning for things to get all right & so that we could meet again & go on living as before. I can't get used to the idea that I should become an American. I won't do it until I'm forced' (707).

One should always be wary of seeing art as the concrete consequence of life events, but it is noticeable that the major works composed during Britten's transition to, and immediate arrival in, North America – *Les illuminations*, the Violin Concerto – end with loss and uncertainty. This is probably at least as likely to be the development of a sensibility allied with modernism. And in any case, in terms of technique, as distinct from what is being expressed (which is what is often seized upon as reflecting external biographical events or their internal consequences), *Les illuminations* in particular represents a highly significant development, about which Britten felt very positive.

'Definitely my Opus 1'

Les illuminations, Op. 18 – settings of Arthur Rimbaud for high voice and string orchestra – was begun while Britten was still in the UK, and two of the songs, 'Being Beauteous' and 'Marine', were given their first performance

---

[4] BC 86.

by Sophie Wyss (for whom they were originally written) in the all-Britten BBC concert shortly before the composer's departure to the United States.

It is of course impossible to know how the work developed in Britten's mind. Attempts to rationalize the steps in the compositional process are an act of imagination rather than the chimera of objective discovery. The process can never be recovered, even by the composer, who will not work in a linear or entirely rational way, but through a mixture of the rational and the intuitive. The impression gained from the compositional history of *Les illuminations* is that Britten assembled the work piecemeal. With the first two songs already completed, he telegrammed Ralph Hawkes to say he had finished 'TWO NEW RIMBAUD SONGS SUITABLE WITH OTHERS FOR PROMENADE PERFORMANCE' (*LL2* 683). Writing to Sophie Wyss he said that these four songs together made a 'much better group' (690). It seems, though, that he was already envisaging a larger work: more than a month before the telegram he had written to Hawkes suggesting a seven-movement work, and this was later reordered and expanded to nine movements.[5]

While we don't know at what point Britten decided upon the work's distinctive musical structure, his statements about his methods (albeit made much later in his career) suggest that he probably had the basic idea from the beginning. That 'basic idea' seems to have been to employ the tritone, the epitome of non-relatedness in music (in tonal contexts, at least), as the most vivid way of projecting the vision and strangeness of Rimbaud's poetry.

The interval of the tritone spans three whole tones – for example, from the note C to D, then to E, and then to F sharp. It can be conceived within the traditional tonal system in two ways, either as an augmented fourth or as a diminished fifth (and thus spelt either C–F sharp, using the example above, or C–G flat). That these are both labelled as adjustments (to the perfect fourth and perfect fifth respectively) is some indication of the tritone's role: it is inherently unstable, demanding resolution. In medieval and Renaissance music it was avoided, being heard as a representation – or perhaps even indicating the presence – of the Devil (*diabolus in musica*). But its instability was particularly valued in the Romantic era; the interval formed the crucial element in chords (such as the diminished seventh, itself consisting of two interlocking tritones, the dominant seventh, various versions of the augmented sixth, and that embodiment of Romantic longing, the 'Tristan' chord) that allowed what Richard Taruskin has described as 'That tandem of unpredictable flexibility at the short range and unerring long-range direction'.[6]

---

[5] See *LL2* 650. The changes to the scheme are tabulated by the editors in *LL2* 652.

[6] Richard Taruskin, *The Oxford History of Western Music*, 5 vols (2nd edn, Oxford; New York: Oxford University Press, 2010), vol. 3 'Music in the Nineteenth Century', 521.

In the twentieth century the tritone was employed by, among others, Bartók as a way of revivifying tonality: his String Quartet No. 5 (1934) and *Music for Strings, Percussion and Celesta* (1936) both use it as the principal 'generator' of musical structure. Britten, too, organizes *Les illuminations* around a tritonal 'dichotomy', between B flat and E. This is presented in its simplest form in the opening song of the work, 'Fanfare', in which the common chords on those notes simply alternate – essentially facing off with increasing vehemence without any possibility of resolution until a third chord is introduced. This is a seventh chord on C, which, in containing both E and B flat, absorbs and neutralizes (which is not to say resolves) the conflict. The dichotomy is then played out in various ways over the ensuing songs until it is reintroduced in a variant of 'Fanfare' in the 'Interlude' between movements V and VII. Again C emerges as a neutralizing force, and forms the tonic for the next two songs, 'Being Beauteous' and 'Parade'. So strong is C at the end of 'Parade' that the move in the next song, 'Départ', to E flat has a profoundly depressive effect. In general, moves up the 'circle of fifths' have a lifting effect while those downwards, like this (it is in fact a shift, rather than a smooth progression, three steps down), have the opposite effect. Britten indicated to Sophie Wyss as she was preparing for the first performance that the 'O Rumeurs et Visions' part of the song 'should bring tears to the eyes of even the program sellers at the back of the hall' (*LL2* 715).

The heightened sensibility leading from the interaction and collision of differently expressed tonalities might have been one of the things that led Britten to describe *Les illuminations* as 'definitely my Opus 1' in a letter to Hawkes (*LL2* 711) – even though he had already said this about *Our Hunting Fathers*. Clearly this set of technical and expressive 'discoveries' trumped those of the earlier work and offered more opportunities for development. Meanwhile the dramatic potentialities of his 'new way' would certainly have ramifications for his work in opera.

A new aspect of *Les illuminations* identified by Philip Brett is its physicality: 'it is difficult to avoid the conclusion that the piece as a whole encapsulates a certain hard-won victory over the distancing effect from the purely corporeal to which British middle-class education was dedicated. It joyously and unashamedly reclaims music as an immediate, physical act.'[7] This is not, in fact, new: both 'Rats Away!' and the 'Dance of Death' in *Our Hunting Fathers* are obvious previous examples of physicality in Britten's music, and there are many more (the outer movements of the Sinfonietta, Op. 1, have a kind of athleticism, for instance). Where Brett certainly has a point is in the eroticism of 'Phrase', with its quietly ecstatic peak at 'et je danse', and the song to which it acts as introduction (the dance itself), 'Antique'. The latter

---

[7] *BBGO.*

was dedicated to Wulff Scherchen, and can easily be read as a portrait ('Graceful son of Pan! About your brow crowned with small flowers and berries move your eyes, precious spheres', and so on[8]). 'Being Beauteous', on the other hand, was dedicated to Pears ('Against a snowfall a Being Beauteous, tall of stature'[9]), though, as Bridcut points out, Britten associated this song with Wulff Scherchen initially too.[10]

If the deeply melancholic ending of *Les illuminations* is brought about chiefly through the manipulation of tonalities, the equivocal, bittersweet ending of the Violin Concerto, Op. 15 (1939) results rather from modal ambiguity. It is normal in common-practice tonality for either the major or the minor form of the tonic triad to be in a position of ascendency (a work is usually in, say, D major or D minor), but here the violin soloist fades out, oscillating – in fact trilling – between the two alternative mediants (the major and minor thirds that define the mode). There had been a degree of modal equivocation in *Our Hunting Fathers*, but here the effect is especially powerful since the tonal centre is not in doubt and the alternative mediants are presented in effect simultaneously.

Les illuminations and the Violin Concerto are very different works, demonstrating Britten's ability to engage imaginatively with a wide range of genres. A further example of his range is a work for piano and string orchestra entitled *Young Apollo*, completed in August 1939. Britten's draft programme note reveals its basis as being the final words of the unfinished *Hyperion* by Keats: ' — and lo! from all his limbs / Celestial —— ' (*BoM* 366), and his letter of 8 December 1939 to Wulff Scherchen indicates that *Young Apollo*, too, is about him (*LL2* 742). Though the work has a few reflective moments, the main impression is of exuberance and vitality, the chromatic 'deflections' from A major being playful rather than destabilizing as in later works – indeed, these deflections serve to point up the idyllic brilliance of the main key when it returns. Perhaps as well as a tribute to all that Britten found attractive in Wulff it is also a portrait of how he himself would have liked to be. The final part of the programme note might be read as an announcement of the arrival of a brilliant new composer:

> The end of one order of Gods has come. Saturn, Hyperion and the other ancient gods, who ruled the world by might and terror, have to make way to the new order, gods of light, youth, beauty and laughter. Apollo, called to be the new god of beauty by Mnemosyne, the old goddess of memory, foresees his destiny; and in one final convulsion throws off his mortal form. He stands before us – the new, dazzling Sun-god, quivering with radiant vitality.

---

[8] The translation is by George Hall in the booklet accompanying Pears and Britten's recording, Decca 417 153-2.
[9] Ibid.
[10] *BC* 102.

It is poignant, therefore, that Britten felt the need to withdraw *Young Apollo* after its first performance (with himself as soloist). While this might have been because of a need to expunge Wulff from his mind, one would like to think that he took this action for primarily musical reasons – despite the brilliance of the work's sonic invention, it is exasperating and tedious in its constant return to A and its one thematic shape. The withdrawal is a reminder that Britten still had a good deal to learn. And perhaps he also recognized that if Beauty were to be a fruitful topic through which to engage his own situation and the contemporary political and cultural climate he needed to explore its dangers as well as its joys.

A number of other works from this period were withdrawn: *A.M.D.G.* for unaccompanied choir, originally assigned the opus number 17; *An Occasional Overture*, originally assigned the opus number 27;[11] and, of course, *Paul Bunyan*. This last was revived by Britten himself (though he had to be persuaded), while the others were brought into the light of day by his Estate after his death, along with numerous items of juvenilia, discarded songs from song-cycles, and so on. Ethical issues surround the resurrection of works that Britten himself was clearly not satisfied with, but such action may be justified in that some, at least, of the revived pieces add a little to what we know of Britten. The composer's judgements regarding withdrawal of his works seem invariably to be right; in general, however, the quality of the works of the American period is impressively high.

To Peter

In an interview with Joseph Cooper, Britten stated that the *Seven Sonnets of Michelangelo*, Op. 22 (1940), the first whole composition written for and dedicated to Pears, completed in the middle of their American sojourn, was the 'principal work' of his American period.[12] It was written for the pair to perform together, and it is impossible to view the settings of love poetry by the homosexual poet as anything other than a declaration of love.

Exactly when Britten and Pears began to view themselves as a couple is difficult to fix with cast-iron certainty. Pears seems to have seen the 'seminal moment' (as Bridcut perhaps rather unfortunately puts it[13]) as being a night during a stay at Grand Rapids in Michigan during 9–19 June 1939. On 9 January 1940 the singer wrote to the composer from New York, while Britten was on tour again, this time in Illinois, 'I shall never forget a certain night in Grand Rapids' (*LL2* 759), and towards the end of Britten's life, in November 1974, asserted that 'it is *you* who have given *me* everything, right from the beginning, from yourself in Grand Rapids'.[14]

---

[11] This was published after Britten's death as *An American Overture*, to distinguish it from the curtain-raiser he composed for the Third Programme also entitled *An Occasional Overture* (1946).
[12] *BoM* 151.
[13] *BC* 94.
[14] *BB* 130.

4. *Britten and Peter Pears at the piano, in Long Island, USA, in 1939.*

However, Bridcut wonders whether as far as Britten was concerned this night might have been 'more an experiment than a consummation of marriage', given that he was still pining for Wulff at the time.[15] He has a persuasive case. In his letter to Wulff of December 1939 Britten declares that 'life here is going on just the same' (which, in terms of personal relationships, was clearly not the case) and goes on to say

> I am playing my 'Young Apollo' which I wrote for the Canadian Broadcasting Corp. – on Columbia on Dec. 20th, sometime in the middle of your night – you know whom that's written about – founded on last lines of Keat's Hyperion [...] O – if all this bloody business would clear up – or if you could come over here. That's what I want most of all. (*LL2* 742)[16]

Pears is not mentioned except in connection with their difficulty in letting their London flat, which 'cost Peter & me untold bother & expense'. Britten

---

[15] *BC* 96.
[16] The ellipsis with square brackets is the editors'. The missing text is provided in *BC*: '– my God, don't I long to see you again' (100).

seems intent on hiding his relationship with Pears: another letter contains the PS 'Peter sends his love, & says he's looking after me – and he certainly is – like a mother hen!' (*LL2* 702), which is as shorn of any suggestion of eroticism as can be imagined. Britten's longing for Wulff finally peters (or Peters) out in the middle of 1942. Wulff though may also have inspired even *Seven Sonnets*. There is evidence that Auden might have introduced Britten to Michelangelo's poetry in the late 1930s, and Wulff Scherchen, in 1989, recalled 'Ben complaining of a "mental block" over a Michael Angelo Sonnet & "putting it away"'. I'm sure I saw the Italian text' (801).

The *Seven Sonnets* is different from the earlier song-cycle *Les illuminations* in more than the obvious fact that the voice is partnered by the piano: it is more loosely organized, without the ramified tonal scheme of the earlier work. In this way the work sets the norm for the song-cycles to come. And if *Les illuminations* engaged with Gallic stylistic traits (the Fauré-like 'Départ'; the Les Six-like aspects of 'Royauté' and 'Marine'), the *Seven Sonnets* engages with the sustained *cantabile* line for which Italian music is so famous. Nowhere more is this the case than in 'Veggio co' bei', which, with its wide leaps and expansive phrases, must have been as much a test for Pears's technique as a vehicle for his musicianship. The song can be thought of as a prime example of 'enriched simplicity' – the employment of simple textures and straightforward materials to sophisticated, and often complex (as distinct from merely complicated), effect.[17]

The cycle ends with a song in D major. Britten seems to have had a thing about that key: by that date his significant works in D major, or those gravitating to it by the end (or ending with it just out of sight), include the Sinfonietta, *Our Hunting Fathers*, the Variations on a Theme of Frank Bridge, the Piano Concerto and the Violin Concerto. The remaining major works of the American period, *Sinfonia da Requiem*, Op. 20 and the String Quartet No. 1, Op. 25, are also D-centred (and D major-concluding). The composer himself was aware of this leaning, having written as follows to his initial hostess in America, Elizabeth Mayer: 'The Quartet is in 4 movements ... & in – would you believe it? – D major!!' (*LL2* 961). No commentator appears yet to have suggested a symbolic meaning; perhaps ideas just happened to come to Britten more often, and in a quality more acceptable to him, in that key.

'Mental perplexities'

That the main American works after *Les illuminations* and the Violin Concerto all end on a positive note belies the increasing doubt and uncertainty in Britten's mind which is revealed in letters to his family and friends in the UK. But his outlook seems to have perked up from July 1941,

---

[17] I have written about this song in some detail in Christopher Mark, 'Simplicity in Early Britten', *Tempo*, 147 (1983), 8–14.

with his and Pears's trip to California – made in an old Ford V8. When, in 1939, they first arrived in New York from Quebec they had stayed at the Amityville home of Elizabeth and William Mayer, whom Pears had met during his tour with the New English Singers.[18] (William Mayer was a psychiatrist, and the house was part of a complex serving a mental institution.) Then in November 1940 Britten and Pears had moved to Brooklyn, to live closer to the hub of the New York creative world. Going west the following summer was in response to an invitation from the piano duo Ethel and Rae Robertson to stay with them in Escondido, north of San Diego.[19] Britten was clearly relieved to breathe the air of the American wide-open spaces. He wrote to his sister Barbara:

> The people are <u>much</u> nicer when you get out of the Eastern cities – & our hearts broke to see everyone looking so English, & all the names sounded Anglo-Saxon – this was mostly in Virginia, Tennessee & Oklahoma. You see, in New York, the percentage of fair hair is very small – & most names are Italian or Jewish, with sprinklings of Polish and Irish. It was such a change. And the people are so simple & honest, compared to the sophisticated scheeming masses of New York. I felt I liked America for the first time! (*LL2* 941)

It wasn't long, though, before he was finding California equally, if not more, uncongenial. In describing Hollywood to Beth towards the end of his stay he confesses, 'I'm abit sick of California – there is a feeling of unreality about it which is not so pleasant as you'd think' (*LL2* 969). The discontent then apparently peaks:

> it's a crazy country, & I don't think I altogether like it. I know old England is a stuffy place, the BBC is horrible, & the plumbing is bad; but there are lots of things about this 'ere place that arn't so good, either. Their driving – their incessant radio – their fat and pampered children – their yearning for culture (to be absorbed in afternoon lectures, now that they can't 'do' Europe) – and above all their blasted stomachs, with their vitamens, their bowel movements (no one ever 'goes' naturally here – only with a good deal of stimulus!), & their bogus medicines. Still they aren't blowing each other to bits so far, & perhaps that's something. (*LL2* 973–4)

Perhaps it is significant that the caveats (such as 'Don't take this tirade too seriously') issued in earlier complaining letters in connection with *Bunyan* are absent. Yet after Britten had returned to the Mayers at Amityville he described California to Beth as a 'lovely enough place', blamed his dislike

---

[18] Pears's meeting with the Mayers and the family's background is detailed by the editors in *LL2* 679–83.

[19] Britten also had a notion, as he wrote to Beth, of going to Mexico 'so as to get on to the labour-quota (you have to go out of the country & then come back, so as to be able to work without hindrance)' (*LL2* 920–21).

of California on his hosts (they were 'selfish, self-indulgent, conceited to an incredible degree'), and told her to consider joining him in the US after the war 'because America I should think will be the place after the war' (*LL2* 992, 994).

Given this degree of confusion – from which he suffered not just on his return from California but throughout his time in America – it is not surprising that he was struck down with illness. This, at least, is Britten's own view. When asked in a 1959 interview if it wasn't the case that he had intended to become an American citizen, he replied: 'True. But the war changed all that. The change wasn't an intellectual one primarily. I don't think I ever consciously reasoned it out. Certainly I underwent a lot of personal tension. Practically all of 1940 I was ill. Outwardly the ailment was infected tonsils. But the real cause was my mental perplexities. It was a frantically difficult position' (*BoM* 173).

His worst period of illness was in February and March 1940, while he was composing *Sinfonia da Requiem* and *Paul Bunyan*: returning from Chicago for the first American performance of his Piano Concerto with a bad cold, possibly flu, he was then struck down by a streptococcal infection. Britten did feel unwell for most of the year (despite having his tonsils removed in October), but it could be argued that the most serious cause of his 'personal tension' did not lie in his indecision about immigration (which Auden saw as the cause of his illness[20]); rather, it lay in his infatuation with Bobby Rothman[21] – which coincided with Britten telling Bobby's father, David Rothman, in late 1941 that he wanted to give up composing and work in his store.[22] As Rothman pointed out to Britten, this seemed an extreme reaction to compositional block – if that was what the thus-far extraordinarily fecund composer was suffering. Perhaps Britten was trying to cope with the horror that this kind of attraction was not a 'phase' but a fundamental part of his make-up, though it seems odd for him to do so by seeking to locate himself as close to the object of his desire as possible. It seems more likely that the statement to Bobby's father was an impulsive cry of anguish.

The means by which Britten got himself out of the 'block' – and around the psychological torment – is outlined in a letter to Peggy Brosa, wife of the violinist Antonio Brosa (who gave the first performance of Britten's Violin Concerto): 'I do hope you're feeling better, Peggy. Your letter sounded very depressed, my dear – I think after a time one gets into a routine of things, and just lives from day to day. That's what has happened to me – I've even started to work again!' (*LL2* 1008). Perhaps the rigorous work schedules of later years – particularly in the 1950s and 60s, when

---

[20] See *LL2* 776.
[21] See the inter-chapter 'Boys'.
[22] *BB* 160.

they escalated to punishing proportions – were actually devised to keep 'mental perplexities' at bay.

Order and Chaos

Auden – who frequently visited the Mayer household even though he was then teaching at the University of Michigan – was aware of Britten's attraction to boys, even if he didn't know about the crush on Bobby Rothman. This is apparent from a letter he wrote to Britten at the end of January 1942, after he'd heard that Britten and Pears had decided to return to the UK. It was one of the first items of Britten's correspondence to be published (in Mitchell's *Britten and Auden in the Thirties*) and has been regarded in much of the subsequent literature as a significant insight into Britten's artistic persona. The key passages are these:

> Goodness and Beauty are the results of a perfect balance between Order and Chaos, Bohemianism and Bourgeois Convention.
>
> Bohemian chaos alone ends in a mad jumble of beautiful scraps; Bourgeois convention alone ends in large unfeeling corpses. [...]
>
> For middle-class Englishmen like you and me, the danger is of course the second. Your attraction to thin-as-a-board-juveniles, i.e. to the sexless and innocent, is a symptom of this. And I am certain too that it is your denial and evasion of the ~~attractions~~ demands of disorder that is responsible for your attacks of ill-health, ie sickness is your substitute for the Bohemian.
>
> Wherever you go you are and probably always will be surrounded by people who adore you, nurse you, and praise everything you do, e.g. Elisabeth, Peter (Please show this to P to whom all this is also addressed). Up to a certain point this is fine for you, but beware. You see, Bengy dear, you are always tempted to make things too easy for yourself in this way, i.e. to build yourself a warm nest of love (of course when you get it, you find it a little stifling) by playing the lovable talented little boy. (*LL2* 1015–16)

Britten's reply, unfortunately lost, would have made fascinating reading. His comeback in terms of composition might have been that even the most bohemian music needs precise control to be both effective and affective (he might have said that about all art). It is the case, though, that the composer avoided subjects which dealt head-on with the bohemian or 'excess', preferring the elaboration of focused ambiguity. Auden's reply to the reply ('to correct a misunderstanding') is equally as interesting as his original letter, if a little more obscure:

> Of course I didnt [*sic*] mean to suggest that your relationship with Peter was on the school boy level. Its danger is quite the reverse, of you both letting the marriage be too caring. (The escape for the paederast is that a marriage is impossible). You understand each other so well, that you will always both be tempted to identify yourselves with each other. (*LL2* 1016)

5. A formal studio portrait of Britten and W. H. Auden, taken at the time of the rehearsals for Paul Bunyan *in New York, April 1941.*

How much of this was really news to Britten is impossible to say. He had suffered already at the hands of critics telling him that his music possessed a surfeit of technique and a deficit of feeling (it was a consistent jibe on both sides of the Atlantic). Even friends like the Canadian composer and transcriber of gamelan music, Colin McPhee, fell in line with this view, writing in a review of the *Seven Sonnets* in 1943 that the songs were 'baroque and pompous show-pieces, pastiches that hold little interest ... there is little if anything personal in this music' (*LL2* 1202). A couple of years earlier McPhee had written an article on Britten that he showed to the composer. In a letter to Elizabeth Mayer, McPhee told her that 'Ben seems to have winced at quite a few passages; I am glad of it.' McPhee outlined to her his concerns which – coincidentally or not – echo those of Auden, concluding that 'If [Ben] is only wanting a career (and I know that is not it), and a career that I know would be very short, then he need not change. But if he wants to survive, to be played with love later on, even during the later years of his life, he must search deeper for a more personal, more *interesting* idiom.'[23]

It is strange that someone of McPhee's evident musicianship should fail to notice what are in fact highly personal traits in the *Seven Sonnets* (and in the Violin Concerto, *Les illuminations* and *Sinfonia da Requiem*, all of which he must have known). But on this occasion Britten seems to have been little concerned. He was always likely to take Auden very seriously, but McPhee's

---

[23] Quoted in 'Eros and Orientalism in Britten's operas', in Philip Brett, *Music and Sexuality in Britten* (Berkeley, CA: University of California Press, 2006), 132.

criticisms were probably seen as no more than a passing personal wound. When Britten was back in the UK he wrote to Elizabeth Mayer about his fate in the States generally: 'Don't worry my dearest if things don't go well for me in the States; I don't, because I know how fickle the musical public is, & how superficial their judgements (although I was a bit grieved by Colin's attack on the Michelangelo Sonnets)' (LL2 1201).

While it would be absurdly reductionist to view the themes of Auden's letters as providing the key to the understanding of Britten's personality, they become increasingly significant. Auden's words certainly seem to have had an effect. Britten appeared, for example, to be responding to the challenge when he wrote to Kit Welford,

> I cannot tell you how much I agree with and admire your letter. I am so pleased that you have thought things out so carefully. From a very different angle I have come to an identical point-of-view (re discipline & obedience) – but in art, as you know, the bias is to the other direction, that of anarchy and romantic 'freedom'. A carefully chosen discipline is the only possible course. (LL2 1021)

The contents of Welford's original communication are not known, but Britten – who earlier in his letter stated baldly, 'luckily, I believe in my work, and so don't fall into the obvious dangers of half-heartedness, which so many artists feel like these days' – would appear to be declaring himself on the side of 'technical skill'. Meanwhile there are echoes of the American psychologist and educationalist Homer Lane (1875–1925) in Auden's belief that stress and tension lay behind Britten's illness. Sherill Tippins points out that Auden had been impressed by Lane's theories in his early twenties, and 'was always insisting that virtually all illness was psychosomatic, the result of the suppression of natural impulses or other psychic or emotional activity'.[24] It can be argued that, especially in the 1960s, Britten took this to heart, and that his final opera, *Death in Venice*, was an exploration of this theme.

Auden's observation that Britten had around him people who adored him, seeking to create for himself 'a warm nest of love', is astute. This tendency of the composer's could no doubt be interpreted as being his attempt to recreate the 'Heaven' of his Lowestoft childhood home. Auden was also right about Britten finding such 'nests' a little stifling: in the middle of 1940 he wrote to Beth, 'Actually one gets a bit tired [of living with the Mayers] – you see the Home is really a small village where everyone knows everyone & everyone's business, & the intrigues & scandals are unbelievable ... And Mrs. Mayer, darling as she is, is inclined to put people's backs up by not being tactful' (LL2 849). When by November that year Britten and Pears had

---

[24] Sherill Tippins, *February House* (London: Pocket Books, 2005), 74; see also Christopher Isherwood on Auden's early poetry in John Haffenden (ed.), *W. H. Auden* (London: Routledge, 1997), 252.

moved to a sort-of artists' commune in Brooklyn, ostensibly 'to be nearer the big city where things go on & jobs are born' (862), Auden was able to see at first hand how Britten coped with the 'demands of disorder' – for the commune presided over by Auden at the ramshackle 7 Middagh St was much more on the bohemian side than the composer and his partner could ultimately take.

The commune was set up by the very well-connected George Davis, owner of the property, who was fiction editor at *Harper's Bazaar*. The residents included Carson McCullers, Gypsy Rose Lee, and Paul and Jane Bowles, as well as Auden and Britten and Pears. Many of Davis's connections – prominent New York artists and musicians such as Copland and Leonard Bernstein, and émigrés including Kurt Weill, Salvador Dalí and Thomas Mann – passed through or were serial visitors.[25] It seems to have been fun at the start, but, as Pears reminisced in 1979, 'after the tremendous warmth and happiness of Amityville, it wasn't quite home. It was filthy, untidy. Just Bohemia' (*LL2* 911). Auden eventually announced a set of rules to try to deal with the various types of chaos,[26] but the house was clearly never going to be Britten and Pears's kind of utopia.

It was during their residence in Middagh Street that *Paul Bunyan* was completed and first performed. The at times strained collaboration with Auden stemmed from the problem that Britten was often provided with a fait accompli rather than having had his advice sought about his musical needs at the earliest stages; the result was that some of the text was unsuitable. This seems to have been a problem too with their collaboration on a Christmas Oratorio project. Auden moved ahead as before with his text (which was eventually published by itself in 1944 as *For the Time Being*),[27] but Britten seems to have got no further than listing the voice-types of the characters. Separated by the Atlantic after Britten returned to the UK, and with the composer turning his mind to other things, Britten and Auden inevitably drifted apart, and this accelerated as Britten recognized his need for a different mode of collaboration with writers – one in which he was firmly in charge.

Auden had hoped that Britten would stay in the US, and clearly believed that that would be his best course of action. Britten had sat at Auden's feet, intellectually speaking, since first meeting him. He had clearly benefited from Auden's pointing him in various literary directions (Michelangelo and Rimbaud were two obviously successful recommendations), and it is probable that some of Britten's political opinions and views on the social usefulness of music were formed or at least strengthened by listening to Auden giving forth. Whether or not the poet had an entirely positive effect

---

[25] For the history of the venture, see Tippins, *February House*, and also *LL2* 863–6 for an extensive editorial note on the household.

[26] Tippins, *February House*, 189–90.

[27] Auden's progress is outlined in *LL2* 1090–95.

6. *7 Middagh Street, New York City, Britten and Pears's home from late 1940 to mid-1941. The date of the photograph is unknown but is believed to be from around this period.*

on Britten's coming to terms with and exploring his sexuality is debatable, but Auden certainly provided a strong point of reference against which Britten could try to define the way he engaged with being gay. Most significantly, however, he provided an exemplar for coherent eclecticism. Locating Auden within the poetic landscape between the two world wars, Peter Childs has noted that

> Alongside his internationalism and his Englishness, his easy use of light verse and complex syntax, it is above all the way that, in terms of sentiment and reference, Auden blends the personal and the public, and the everyday with the esoteric, that makes him seem both indebted to Eliot and markedly different from him; such that in his

autobiographical 'Letter to Lord Byron' Auden can mention Disney, the Great North Road, Baden-Powell, Sunlight Soap, Kodak cameras, and even quantum theory, without making the reader feel that the images jar or are being used to suggest the degeneration of culture.[28]

During his 'Auden Years' Britten had drawn on a range of sources, many seemingly irreconcilably disparate, which would surprise anyone knowing only the works from his time at the RCM. Sometimes the eclecticism doesn't work: the jazzy number at the end of *On this Island*, for example, is too much of a throw-away, and *Paul Bunyan* ends up being rather less than the sum of its parts. But the eclectic enterprises in which Britten is in sole control – the Variations on a Theme of Frank Bridge, the Violin Concerto, *Les illuminations*, the *Seven Sonnets*, and other major American scores which wear their eclecticism more lightly (such as the String Quartet No. 1 and the *Sinfonia da Requiem*) – are impressively integrated.

It is one of a number of contradictions of this period that even while Britten's compositional crisis was supposedly at its peak, he was already contemplating one of the most challenging undertakings for a composer: opera. His fluency, which never seriously deserted him, suggests a core confidence in his ability. It is as if his professed doubts were a way of perpetuating Bridge's check on his professionalism, an internalized re-enactment of the compositional lessons in which he would be sent to the other side of the room while Bridge played over his latest effort and demanded whether he really meant what he'd written.[29]

The stimulus for his first 'proper' opera – the siren call of East Anglia delivered through George Crabbe's poetry – is one of the most famous stories of Britten's career. In July 1941, while on his and Pears's Californian excursion, he wrote to Elizabeth Mayer: 'We've just re-discovered the poetry of George Crabbe (all about Suffolk!) & are very excited – maybe an opera one day ...!!' (*LL2* 961). He had come across an article by E. M. Forster on the poet in *The Listener*. Whether or not the decision to return home really was instant, Britten later recalled it as such. He reflected in a speech and in a radio programme in 1964 and 1965 respectively, 'I suddenly realized where I belonged and what I lacked' and 'in a flash I realized two things: that I must write an opera, and where I belonged' (962).

The opera – the premiere of which was to be the defining event in Britten's career – was commissioned in February 1942 by the Russian émigré conductor Serge Koussevitzky, who had performed *Sinfonia da Requiem*. Its topic was the events surrounding a relatively minor character in Crabbe's *The Borough*, the fisherman Peter Grimes. The scenario was sketched out as he and Pears returned to the UK across the U-Boat-infested Atlantic, having finally secured a passage on the MS *Axel Johnson* leaving on 16 March 1942.

[28] Peter Childs, *The Twentieth Century in Poetry: A Critical Survey* (London: Routledge, 1999), 115.
[29] See 'Britten Looking Back', in *BoM* 250–53.

Collaboration

The image of the composer locked away in his or her ivory tower emerging only occasionally into the concert hall for the first performance of the latest masterwork is not entirely false: composers do need protracted stretches of time to work on large-scale works, and twentieth-century English composers, at any rate, have tended to seek out quiet rural retreats where they can immerse themselves in their latest project. This was the case with Elgar, Vaughan Williams and Tippett (who all embedded themselves in the English countryside from time to time), as well as Walton (who emigrated to the Italian island of Ischia) and, more recently, Peter Maxwell Davies (who moved to the Orkney Isles in the 1970s) and Birtwistle (who spent a while on the inner Hebridean island of Raasay and in rural France before settling in Wiltshire). But all these composers recognized music as an inherently collaborative activity, involving not only what Britten referred to as 'this holy triangle of composer, performer and listener',[1] but also poets (living or dead), librettists, stage and costume designers, and producers. (The list can extend to include record producers, publishers, agents, administrators, and so on.) Britten himself withdrew to a compositional haven from time to time, increasingly so during the late 1950s and 60s as his public profile rose. But in accepting work with the GPO Film Unit, various theatre groups and BBC radio when he left the RCM, he apprenticed himself to a type of working that was to dominate his career. For while the role of music is different in opera from that in film and the theatre, and the behaviour of the composer correspondingly so, Britten must have learnt much about strategies of negotiation and how to navigate the unpredictable currents of the collaborative process.

Britten was very much the junior partner in his film and theatre work. When he attempted to work with one of his senior partners from those contexts, W. H. Auden, on *Paul Bunyan*, the experience was not always as productive as he wished. This must have convinced him that, for future ventures, he would need to have greater control. Later, in 1963, when asked by his interviewer Murray Schafer why he hadn't worked with Auden subsequently, he said:

---

[1] See 'On Receiving the First Aspen Award', *BoM* 261.

BRITTEN: Since 1942 we have not been together very often and I couldn't ask anyone to prepare a libretto for me without being in on it myself from the start.

SCHAFER: You like to help shape the libretto yourself?

BRITTEN: I have to. I get lots of libretti in the post but I have never accepted one. A few of the ideas are attractive enough, but I have to be in on it from the beginning. (*BoM* 225)

This was the case from his first 'proper' opera, *Peter Grimes*, Op. 33 (1945), onwards: it was Britten who held the commissions and 'drove' the process. It would be inaccurate to characterize him as a control freak, for he was, after all, content – even eager – for others to conduct the first performances of some of his large-scale works.[2] But there is also no doubting who had the final say in all matters relating to his works. In a short essay on his second opera, *The Rape of Lucretia*, Op. 37 (1946), he espouses what seems to be an equal partnership between composer and poet but makes it clear that he sees the duty of the librettist to adjust to the composer and not the other way around:[3] at no point does he suggest that the composer should have to rework his music to accommodate literary niceties. This shouldn't surprise us, since the ready acceptance that experiencing opera in translation (or on the radio or via an audio recording) doesn't involve too great a degradation of the dramatic experience would seem to confirm the primacy of music.

Britten's notion of the librettist's role is reinforced in discussions between the various collaborators on *Albert Herring*, Op. 39 (1947) and *Billy Budd*, Op. 50 (1951), broadcast on the BBC Third Programme and transcribed by Kildea in *Britten on Music*.[4] In the case of *Herring* the discussion involves Britten, the librettist Eric Crozier, and the designer John Piper. It lays out what must have become a model for each subsequent opera's development: planning a 'rough shape', writing the libretto (or a large part of it), discussion, rewriting, and composing the music with adjustments to the libretto as necessary.[5] Britten sums up the intent thus: 'I suppose in a way we've tried in this opera to make every element in it as good as every other – to treat the scenery, the libretto, the acting, the production, the orchestral playing, and the singing, equally seriously' (*BoM* 74).

---

[2] See the inter-chapter 'Performing'.
[3] See *BoM* 78–9.
[4] See *BoM* 67–74 and 194–207 respectively. The programmes were broadcast the night before the first performance in the case of *Albert Herring*, and the night before the first performance of the revised, two-act version in the case of *Billy Budd*.
[5] See *BoM* 68–9.

The Third Programme discussion on *Budd* gives the impression that the librettists worked well together. E. M. Forster, the co-librettist, says '… if you read the history of collaboration – I think books have been written about it – it seems a lamentable theme. But in our case it was nothing but pleasure' (*BoM* 200). And yet a significant disagreement between Britten and Forster arises concerning who is the central character. For Britten, 'Billy always attracted me, of course – the radiant, young figure … but I think I must admit that Vere, who has what seems to me the main moral problem of the whole work, round whom the drama was going to centre …' (197). At this point Britten either peters out or is interrupted by Crozier, who asks, 'What do you feel, Morgan?' Forster responds, 'I tend to think Billy the central figure. He names the opera, and I think I consider the things from his point of view' (197–8). The plot revolves around the Vere–Billy axis to the extent that one might argue that together they represent 'the central character'. That said, the story arises out of Vere's recollections and ends with his reflections, and to this extent the work would seem to be essentially about him.

Whether the difference of opinion regarding the central character was aired during their work together on the opera is not known, but Forster's correspondence shows that he was not slow to criticize Britten's music when he felt the need – when, for example, he found defects in the music Britten had written for Claggart's aria, 'O beauty, O handsomeness, goodness':

> It is *my* most important piece of writing and I did not, at my first hearings, feel it sufficiently important musically … I want *passion* – love constricted, perverted, poisoned, but nevertheless *flowing* down its agonizing channel; a sexual discharge gone evil. Not soggy depression or growling remorse. I seemed turning from one musical discomfort to another, and was dissatisfied. I looked for an aria perhaps, for a more recognizable form. I liked the last section best, and if it is extended so that it dominates, my vague objections may vanish. 'A longer line, a firmer melody' – exactly. (*LL3* 618)

This didn't go down well with Britten, who presumably regarded Forster's criticisms as overstepping the mark and skewing what he saw as the proper relationship between operatic collaborators. Crozier had to hose things down, and while relations between Forster and Britten were cordial enough for them to meet at Britten's home a couple of months before the first performance, Britten wasn't at ease.[6]

---

[6] See the letter to Erwin Stein, *LL3* 677–8.

Britten wrote to both Forster and Crozier immediately after the first performance of *Budd* thanking them for what he referred to respectively as 'incomparably the finest libretto ever' (*LL3* 682) and 'the finest libretto I've ever heard or read' (698). It was probably to be expected that the collaboration with Forster would be a one-off, but for whatever reason the relationship with Crozier was at an end, too. Imogen Holst reports in her diary for 18 February 1953, while Britten was at work on his next opera, *Gloriana*, Op. 53 (1953), that he 'looked very tired and dreaded his evening with Eric ... He said he needed a stiff drink before Eric came'; and that on the next day 'He was still feeling depressed about Eric when I went down to begin the morning's work'.[7]

The librettist for *Gloriana* was William Plomer, and he and Myfanwy Piper – whose first project with Britten was *The Turn of the Screw*, Op. 54 (1954) – were to be librettists for the remaining operas. It is apparent from the extant correspondence that Britten's collaboration with both was the most congenial of his career, perhaps because both Plomer and Piper felt secure enough to offer strong suggestions (which they did, and which were often taken up) and because they recognized that their role was to provide the composer with what he wanted. During the composition of *Death in Venice*, Op. 88 (1973) one exchange between Piper and Britten, regarding the voice of Apollo that is introduced during the ballet section of Act I and the dream sequence in Act II, sums up the tone and character of their working relationship, and also shows Pears's capacity to make crucial contributions:

MP to BB 28 February 1972:
There is no doubt in my mind that Aschenbach was a devotee of Apollo – that Apollo is the God whom he puts up against Dionysus and that Tadzio therefore also can and does represent Apollo in his mind so that in his distraught state a voice that could be Tadzio's would be dramatically right if you think we can get away with it. I'm not pressing it – just giving you to think. (*BPL*)

BB to MP 6 March 1972:
I think your reasoning re Tadzio - Apollo is very convincing, altho' I am still worried by a possible confusion in the audience's mind. I still like the idea of a boy's voice there; but Peter has had a stranger idea, but possibly a better one

[7] Christopher Grogan (ed.), *Imogen Holst: A Life in Music* (Woodbridge: Boydell Press, 2007), 204, 205.

– why not a counter-tenor – colder, not manly or womanly, & a sound that hasn't been used before. What do you think? (*BPL*)

Britten's collaborator on the set designs from *The Rape of Lucretia* onwards (and, in *Gloriana*, on the costumes, too) was Myfanwy Piper's husband, the painter John Piper. Apparently Britten told him, 'I can't write the music until I can visualize the action!'[8] Colin Graham, who produced *Noye's Fludde* (1957) and the operas after *A Midsummer Night's Dream* (1960), is reported as saying that Britten had an 'ever-open mind to ideas' and 'never had a pre-conceived notion about how an opera would look'; however, 'it was important for the composer to know before composition what the original concept was likely to be. Hence the intensive early discussions.'[9] Graham's role in assisting with Britten's rethinking of his approach to music drama for *Curlew River*, Op. 71 (1964) bears this out. He was charged with developing an approach to movement that recreated, but was not directly derived from, the Nō tradition on which the work was based, and with developing a set that could accommodate the co-ordination of the conductorless ensemble Britten was employing. Graham constructed a model of the set and needed to have it by him while Britten was composing the work

> so that we could decide exactly where people were going to stand, and it was so important to decide who was going to lead the music at every point ... if it was the viola, the viola had to be able to see the Ferryman, or whatever, or they had to be able to see each other to be able to get the cues from the singers.[10]

Graham worked on and off, from 1965 to 1968, on a libretto for *Anna Karenina*, with considerable input too from William Plomer – but Britten abandoned the project before composing a note. This did not, however, dampen Graham's enthusiasm for working with the composer, and he played a significant role in envisaging ways of adapting Mann's novella, *Death in Venice*, for the stage for what was to be Britten's final opera. In the event not all the ideas were taken up, but some of them ended up characterizing the theatrical approach, suggesting that in Graham and the Pipers Britten had finally found his ideal collaborators.

[8] Alan Blyth, *Remembering Britten* (London: Hutchinson, 1981), 29.
[9] Ibid., 118.
[10] From an interview with Keith Grant quoted by Philip Reed in his introduction to *LL5*, xxxvi.

THREE

OPERA AND FESTIVAL (1943–1960)

It has recently been suggested that Britten was worried about being drafted into the US army if he stayed in America, and that this was one of the reasons – if not the reason – why he and Pears decided to return to the UK.[1] Whether this was the case or not, he would have been in little doubt that, as a conscientious objector, he would face considerable resentment and hostility when he arrived home, where a 'Battle of Britten' was being waged in his absence.

This phrase appears to have been coined as a musical rallying-cry by Ernest Newman in a supportive critique of the Violin Concerto in the *Sunday Times* in May 1941. But it soon acquired political and moral connotations when a letter to the newspaper complained of Britten's sheltering in America while other English composers were 'directing all their endeavours' to the war effort.[2] In September 1940 Ralph Hawkes had already warned Britten, 'There is no doubt at all that we are going to have difficulty in getting performances of your works and caustic comment has been passed on your being away' (*LL2* 870). Public signs of resentment peaked in the correspondence pages of the principal organ of musical opinion in the UK, *The Musical Times*, from June to October 1941, under the headline 'English Composer Goes West'. It was initiated by a correspondent signing himself 'E R Lewis (Pilot-Officer)'.

> Why should special favour be given to works which are not of first rank when they come from men who have avoided national service, and when so many British artists have suffered inroads upon their work so as to preserve that freedom which, musically, they have not

---

[1] See Brian McMahon, 'Why Did Britten Return to Wartime England?', in Lucy Walker (ed.), *Benjamin Britten: New Perspectives on his Life and Work* (Woodbridge: Boydell Press, 2009), 174–85.
[2] *LL2* 958–9.

yet enjoyed to the full? It is not encouraging to see others thriving on a culture which they have not the courage to defend.[3]

Leading the defence was one Gerald Cockshott: 'If this composer fulfils his early promise, posterity will not care a brass farthing how he behaved or did not behave as a member of society. They will rather thank their stars that Mr. Britten had the sense to act as any government with a genuine regard for art would have *made* him act.' To this the Editor riposted: '… there are even worse fates than being unable to go on living and "composing in America," and one of them may be the consciousness of having saved one's art and skin at the cost of failure to do one's duty.'[4] After further exchanges in the next issue, Cockshott had one final say before the correspondence was closed: 'I had thought that tolerance of unpopular viewpoints and the freedom of the individual conscience were the very things that all of us wish to maintain. If so, there can be no harm in pointing out that Freedom, like Charity, begins at home. As Feste so admirably remarks in another context: "Minorities deserve more consideration than they get."'[5]

In the event the outrage made little impact. Britten's impression a couple of weeks after arriving back in 1942, conveyed in a letter to Elizabeth Mayer, was that 'So far people have all been nice to me, and there has been no suggestion of vindictiveness' (*LL2* 1037). Some voices were still raised against his participation in musical life, Boult and the BBC staff conductor Clarence Raybould among them,[6] but in general Britten's conscientious objection and time in the US don't seem to have hampered him. He registered along with Pears as a conscientious objector as soon as he returned to the UK and faced a tribunal the following month. He was ordered to non-combatant duties in the Army, but his Appeal against this allowed him to go about his normal business.[7]

By this time Boult, as music director at the BBC, had received an enthusiastic note from the assistant director Julian Herbage, who had heard Britten play through various of his American works at Boosey & Hawkes's premises only five days after the composer had landed at Liverpool: 'My whole impression is that during the last couple of years Britten has grown greatly in stature as a composer and has now found a simple individual and clear cut style. With his extraordinary mastery of technique one looks for most important if not great things from him in the future' (*LL2* 653). The works played included the *Sinfonia da Requiem* (in a two-piano version with Pears playing second piano) and the *Seven Sonnets of Michelangelo*. Britten told Elizabeth Mayer that the latter 'made a great impression' (1037).

---

[3] *The Musical Times*, 82 (June 1941), 234.
[4] *The Musical Times*, 82 (Aug. 1941), 308–9.
[5] *The Musical Times*, 82 (Oct. 1941), 376.
[6] *SB* 66–7.
[7] Britten's statements to the two Tribunals are reproduced in *BoM* 40–41.

Once Britten made up his mind to return to the UK, he became engaged with things English as never before, and turned wholeheartedly to the setting of English texts. That this was to be Englishness on his own terms is signalled by the set of *Folksong Arrangements. Vol. 1: British Isles*, a selection of which was first performed in Michigan in November 1941. They struck a very different (knowingly distanced) relationship with the originals than was typical of the then flagship of musical Englishness, and Britten's old compositional punchbag, Ralph Vaughan Williams. The first two 'original' works to celebrate the re-embracing of the English word, *A Ceremony of Carols*, Op. 28 and *Hymn to St Cecilia*, Op. 27, were completed or largely composed on the Atlantic crossing. If Hawkes and Herbage had heard these they would have recognized a consolidation of the achievements of the works they did hear, but also a striking new tack.

It is probable that Britten started work on the *Hymn to St Cecilia* for unaccompanied chorus – his last major setting of Auden – at around the time he came across Crabbe in California in 1941, though the poet had been working on the text during the previous year. Britten had composed part of the work by the time he left US shores and completed it during the crossing. The music is among his most euphonious, with triads dominating the harmony and with choral textures airily transparent. As in *Les illuminations*, the tonal structure revolves around two triads that are not related in a traditional way, though here the emphasis is not so much on conflict as on ambivalence: the triads concerned, C major and E major, have a note (E) in common. The work begins with an equilibrium between the two, but a tendency for C to inflect E emerges, crystallizing with particular poignancy in the setting of what might be thought of as the text's punchline, Auden's sermonizing injunction to Britten, 'O wear your tribulation like a rose'. Though the poem is ostensibly about music, it is also about loss of innocence and – it seems clear since the publication of Auden's letter to Britten of January 1942 – the balance between 'Bohemianism and Bourgeois Convention'.

If the *Hymn to St Cecilia* is to a certain extent the completion of unfinished business, *A Ceremony of Carols*, begun during the crossing, is more representative of the rapprochement with things English, in that it forges connections with not only the English past (the setting of medieval texts, and the use of plainsong for the framing processional and recessional) but also Britten's own past (a return to the subject-matter of *A Boy was Born*). *Ceremony* was completed in October 1942, though 'That Yongë Child' and the Interlude for harp were not added until mid-1943. While the work is usually associated with boys' voices, it was actually conceived for women. Apparently a modest work, it is nonetheless thoroughly representative of its composer in its placing of a familiar tonal vocabulary in new contexts, in its highly imaginative textures (particularly striking is the dizzyingly exhilarating triple canon at a quaver's distance in 'This little babe'), and in the way in which telling expressive effects are derived from simple means.

The texts of *Ceremony* would have raised few of the eyebrows of those who were following Britten's work, but those of the *Serenade*, Op. 31 for tenor, horn and strings (composed partly when he was in hospital with measles in March and April 1943) might well have done: a vein of romanticism and pastoralism is on display here that is strikingly at odds with the politically charged contemporaneity of Auden's verses for *Our Hunting Fathers* and *On this Island*. Described by Britten to Elizabeth Mayer as 'not important stuff, but quite pleasant, I think' (*LL2* 1144), the *Serenade* quickly began to rival *Les illuminations* in terms of its success with critics and public alike.[8] It is not, in fact, all 'quite pleasant', and is quite important in a number of ways. The least 'pleasant' song is the setting of Blake's 'O Rose, thou art sick', with its marshalling of the major–minor third as a symbol of corrupted innocence, though this could be said to be challenged by the nightmarish visions of 'Lyke-Wake Dirge', into which 'O Rose' directly leads. If this is Britten at his most theatrically brilliant (certainly it is the song in which the horn part, written for the legendary Dennis Brain, appears to reach its peak of difficulty), the final song, a setting of Keats's *Sonnet to Sleep*, is no less virtuosic – and not entirely pleasant, either, in its musical enacting of the subject's distillation of the day's troubles and anxieties before, with the final chord, sleep is at last bestowed.

The *Serenade* received its first performance in October 1943, a month after another new work, *Rejoice in the Lamb*, Op. 30 (a setting of extracts from Christopher Smart's *Jubilate Agno*), was premiered during the celebrations to mark the fiftieth anniversary of the consecration of St Matthew's Church, Northampton. Like *A Ceremony of Carols*, it is ostensibly a modest work, but it achieves an emotional weight and musical significance far beyond its apparent limitations. The solo numbers – about the beauty of Smart's Cat Jeoffry, the valour of the Mouse, and the language of Flowers – draw on Britten's gift for deft characterization honed in his incidental music for the GPO, the BBC, and the theatre companies he had worked for, while the 'Silly Fellow' chorus has frequently been viewed as a precursor of the vehement choral 'pursuit' music of the final stages of *Peter Grimes*. The work's astonishing range is completed by the exhilaration of the faster choruses and the inner ecstasy of the Purcell-inspired concluding 'Halleluiah'.

Britten hadn't begun compositional work on *Peter Grimes* by the time the *Serenade* and *Rejoice in the Lamb* were performed, but was working on the text with his librettist, Montagu Slater. That some musical ideas would have been forming, if not much in the way of actual notes, seems

---

[8] See *LL2* 1175 for several very positive critical notices.

likely. While it would be misleading to regard any of the works of this time as being studies for the opera – not least because setting pre-existing poetry is rather different from collaborating with a librettist in moulding a text from the word go – it would be odd if Britten hadn't taken opportunities to flex some of the muscles needed for opera when they arose. The passages of arioso in the *Serenade* and *Rejoice in the Lamb* and the dramatic scena of 'Silly Fellow' in the latter (which has often been regarded as a mini-'Mad Scene') are examples. But this amounts to fine-tuning: much of the required technique was already in place, and Britten had the experience of *Bunyan* – things that worked, things that didn't – to draw upon.

'An enormous commitment'

It is easy in retrospect to underplay the magnitude of the achievement of Britten's first venture into opera, since the number of operas in his œuvre leads one to assume he had a natural feeling for them. The genre was not totally alien to British composition before this time: Stanford, Holst, Vaughan Williams, Delius and Ethyl Smyth all wrote them, and there was the remarkable case of Rutland Boughton, who founded an opera festival at Glastonbury (modest of means though it was). But native opera was not a priority of the public, performers or administrators, and – despite the achievements of Holst's and Vaughan Williams's chamber operas, *Sāvitri* and *Riders to the Sea* respectively (the latter being particularly fine) – offerings from British composers had not been of the highest level. As is the nature of operatic production, *Grimes* was a team effort. The extraordinary success of the first performances relied on the producer, singers, orchestra, conductor (Reginald Goodall, later to be lauded as one of the finest mid-century Wagner conductors) and administrators all working to the limit of their capacity – not least Pears, in the title role, who was not particularly experienced in opera. He had had a few roles only with Sadler's Wells, the company putting on *Grimes*, which might explain why the part was originally conceived for a baritone. But only the most extreme of postmodern positions would deny the centrality of the composer's part in this most collaborative of musical genres; it is ultimately the quality of what the composer produces that determines the opera's success (or otherwise).

The odd comment from Britten suggests a laissez-faire attitude towards the enterprise – for example, this to Pears two days into the actual composition: 'I don't know whether I shall ever be a good opera composer, but it's wonderful fun to try once in a way!' (*LL2* 1181). But a letter to Henry Wood written a month earlier, explaining that he had nothing to offer him for the 1944 Proms because he was 'just embarking on an enormous commitment – the writing of a full-length opera' (1180), reveals the true sense of what he was trying to do. Brett suggests the venture was a deliberate attempt by Britten to position himself as the leading British composer,[9] and given his competitive nature, this seems entirely plausible. Brett goes on to note, though, that 'the risk of failure was greater, as Britten was aware'.

The degree of confidence required of the composer, and generally displayed by him in his correspondence during the period of the opera's composition, is strikingly at odds with the apparently crippling lack of self-confidence he exhibited only a couple of years earlier. This adds weight to the notion that these attacks of self-doubt were the drastic means (a process of self-abnegation and recovery) by which Britten tried to hold himself to the standards to which he had aspired since becoming Bridge's pupil. It is hard to take at face value his statement in an interview with Alan Blyth in 1970 that 'It never occurred to me that the opera would work. My only other operatic experience until then had been in America with *Paul Bunyan*. This had proved disastrous – the wrong piece in the wrong place – and so I had no confidence about *Grimes*.'[10] During such a long, complex project there were inevitably a few moments of doubt. In March 1943, nine months before starting to write the notes, he wrote to Pears that 'I am going to do lots of work on P. Grimes today, to see what really is wrong with it', and 'I'm beginning to feel that Montagu may not be the ideal librettist' (*LL2* 1123–4). But the following excerpt displays a high level of motivation:

> I am sure it isn't <u>fundamentally</u> hopeless, there are too many things I like about it. For one thing it goes <u>naturally</u> into operatic form – it doesn't embarrass me to think of those people, singing, & singing English. And another, I see so clearly what kind of music I want to write for it, & I <u>am</u> interested in the people & the situations, & interested in a musical way. It isn't often that one can get an opera scheme that comes so near what one wants. (*LL2* 1124)

The only other negative comment came six months into composition, again to Pears: 'My bloody opera stinks, & that's all there is to it.' Yet even this is immediately ameliorated: 'But I dare say that I shall be able to de-odourise it before too long – or I'm hoping so' (*LL2* 1203).

Britten said to Blyth that 'at that time such an off-beat story was hardly thought right for opera', and his correspondence showed signs of apprehension: in March 1943 he wrote to Enid Slater, 'the more I think of P. Grimes the more I like it & get excited over it. The trouble is that I don't think anyone'll be able to bear it on the stage!',[11] and in July 1944 he confided to Elizabeth Mayer that 'It is becoming a bigger affair than I expected and so topical as to be unbearable in spots!' (*LL2* 1211). But these are rare instances, and his note to Christopher Isherwood, who had been approached as

---

[9] See *BBGO*.

[10] Quoted in Philip Brett, *Benjamin Britten: Peter Grimes* (Cambridge: Cambridge University Press, 1983), 91.

[11] Quoted in Philip Reed, 'A *Peter Grimes* Chronology, 1941–1945', in Paul Banks (ed.), *The Making of Peter Grimes: Essays and Studies* (Woodbridge: Boydell Press, 2000), 27.

possible librettist at the earliest stages, is more typical: 'I know that as it stands, P.G. is no more than a rather bloodthirsty melodrama; but it has the elements of what I want in an opera, and we are surely getting nearer to a serious plot.'[12] But, as Michael Wilcox has observed, it does seem remarkable that a desperately grim story – full of cruelty, injustice and various kinds of dysfunction, with sympathy being sought from the audience for an increasingly psychotic central character whose behaviour towards those trying to help him is frequently unwarranted and often vicious – 'should triumph with audiences in a starving, blitzed and bankrupt country at the end of five years of total war'.[13]

Wilcox's study is one of several that see the opera arising out of Britten's sexual nature. The first to do so was Philip Brett's article 'Britten and Grimes' in *The Musical Times* of December 1977,[14] though in the 1983 book that grew out of this he stresses that 'My ultimate concern is the social experience of oppression and its effects in the writing of *Peter Grimes*, not Britten's sexual preference'.[15] Indeed, in discussing the development of the libretto from the scenario sketched out largely by Pears while Britten was at work on *Hymn to St Cecilia* and *A Ceremony of Carols*, Brett highlights the pruning of what he identifies as homo-erotic elements and Grimes's obsession with his father – elements which, he convincingly argues, had to be removed so that the work 'should not be misinterpreted as a "pathological" study'[16] and could work successfully as allegory. One of the most striking changes is logged by Claire Seymour.[17] In the Act II scene 1 confrontation between Ellen Orford and Peter concerning the bruise Ellen finds on the boy's neck, the following lines appeared in the sketch:

ELLEN: Peter tell me one thing, where
Young stranger got his bruise and weals
PETER: Out of my true affection.

This is replaced in the final version with:

ELLEN: Peter, tell me one thing,
Where the youngster got that ugly bruise?
PETER: Out of the hurly burly

Brett sees the opera as an allegory, and Richard Taruskin argues persuasively that 'some level of allegorical interpretation seems necessary if the opera is to succeed in its moral, and even its musical, objective. For

---

[12] Ibid., 24.

[13] Michael Wilcox, *Benjamin Britten's Operas* (Bath: Absolute Press, 1997), 27.

[14] Reproduced in Brett, *Benjamin Britten: Peter Grimes*, 180–89; also in Philip Brett, *Music and Sexuality in Britten* (Berkeley, CA: University of California Press, 2006), 11–33.

[15] Brett, *Benjamin Britten: Peter Grimes*, 192.

[16] Ibid., 196.

[17] Claire Seymour, *The Operas of Benjamin Britten: Expression and Evasion* (Woodbridge: Boydell and Brewer, 2004), 49.

the music has painted Grimes as an innocent man, and yet he perishes as a guilty one.'[18] Brett noted that the most significant aspect of the allegory

> had to do with 'internalization', the classic form of oppression. Those who do not have full status in society come to believe the low opinion others have of them: Grimes's fate is ultimately determined not simply by his isolation but by his capitulation to Borough opinion … Grimes internalizes society's judgment of him and enters the self-destructive cycle that inevitably concludes with his suicide.[19]

The audience is encouraged 'onside' with Grimes from his very first appearance, in the Prologue, during which we see him being harassed (the coroner, Swallow, constantly interrupts him before he manages to finish his phrases) and unable to secure the opportunity of clearing his name, as Grimes himself points out. The musical characterization – our window into Grimes's inner being – is crucial here. It is remarkably deft, swiftly establishing (at this point and in the opening scene of Act I) the character of individuals and of the Borough as a collective. The sure-footedness of the pacing, the intercutting and so on, keeps the audience involved, as does the adoption of a musical language that, while rooted in traditional tonality, constantly reworks it. But perhaps the surest sign that Britten is in his *métier* is his being prepared to undermine the role of music in the service of drama: in the work's latter stages he allows the music to disintegrate entirely so that Balstrode's spoken instruction to Grimes to drown himself is shocking in its puncturing of what, in the opera house, we accept as reality. It is a bold step for a composer to take, and is one instance of Britten's willingness to take risks.

The allotting of key moments of the drama to music of apparent simplicity is another such instance, though he had been taking this particular risk since the beginning of his career. Examples in *Grimes* include the protagonist's 'Great Bear' aria and the women's ensemble 'From the gutter' – which is a reminder that, in British society, women have suffered (and continue to suffer) oppression also. Such instances repay Britten's investment in 'enriched simplicity', his employment of simple textures and straightforward materials to sophisticated effect. The opera is a triumph, too, in his taking up of two other risky compositional 'positions': his rapprochement with tonal structuring (the kind of tensions explored in *Les illuminations*, in particular) and his eclecticism, both of which are harnessed to powerful dramatic ends. These were risky not so much in terms of audience engagement (which both positions proved to further) but in terms of being dismissed critically – on the grounds of a retreat into the past on the one hand and a lack of stylistic integration on the other.

---

[18] Richard Taruskin, *The Oxford History of Western Music*, 5 vols (2nd edn, Oxford; New York: Oxford University Press, 2010), vol. 5 'Music in the Late Twentieth Century', 247.
[19] *BBGO*.

7. The 'Prologue' from Peter Grimes, from the first production in June 1945:
Mr Swallow (Owen Brannigan) stands at a table addressing Peter Grimes (Peter Pears) among the crowd.

Britten might have been encouraged to take up his grim tale, and stick with it, by the example of the even more bleak *Wozzeck* (at least *Grimes* has moments of light relief in the banter of the Borough). It is clear that Berg's opera provided a model for Britten's own: the central characters in both are anti-heroes who drown by their own hand; both operas are cyclic in a sense; both contain an important pub scene; and both contain orchestral interludes that paint psychological portraits of the protagonist (according to Taruskin these are in both scores 'vehicle[s] of manipulative authorial commentary'[20]). In addition, both operas are organized into 'numbers' – arias, ensembles, and so on: 'The classical practice of separate numbers that crystallize and hold the emotions', as Britten puts it in his programme note, contrasting this with 'the Wagnerian theory of "permanent melody"' (*BoM* 50). This might be seen as a consequence of Britten's liking for 'characteristic' music in the 1930s (the Variations on a Theme of Frank Bridge, for instance) and, at a more fundamental level, his tendency to compose all his music, whatever the genre, in sections differentiated by texture and harmonic process. It also suggests the influence of Verdi (the 'mad' scene has a clear resonance with the Italian tradition, too). But the influence Britten himself was most keen to stress was that of Purcell, whom he upheld as a model of the setting of English. His example seems most present in the arioso passages, though there is little that actually sounds like him; it may be that Britten's reference to Purcell was principally designed to establish a connection with the greatest previous English composer for the genre, and to suggest the possibility of establishing opera as a major force in British musical life. Other models that have been suggested include Shostakovich's *Lady Macbeth of the Mtsensk District* (1930–32) and Gershwin's *Porgy and Bess* (1935).[21]

The press reaction to *Grimes*, though not entirely uncritical, was very positive,[22] and the opera's pulling-power can be gauged by examining Sadler's Wells's records of box-office receipts, which show that the production held its own against those perennial draw-cards, *La bohème* and *Madama Butterfly*.[23] Sadler's Wells, though, was not so easily won over. Some difficulties arose with the administration and some of the performers: as Britten wrote in a letter to Rutland Boughton, 'there has been a big bust-up in the company, & the Governors of the Wells have sided with the "opposition" to Grimes, & so it doesn't seem likely that it will be revived there' (*LL3* 105). It seems that, as well as simply disliking the music, some of

---

[20] Taruskin, 'Music in the Late Twentieth Century', 241.
[21] Britten wrote a short note on *Lady Macbeth* in the first issue of *World Film News* after hearing a concert performance in 1936, and in a tribute to Shostakovich written thirty years later referred to that experience as 'a knockout' – see *BoM* 17 and 300–301. Parallels with *Porgy* are outlined in *LL2* 638.
[22] The main notices are reproduced in *LL2* 1253–65.
[23] See Banks (ed.), *The Making of Peter Grimes*, xvi–xviii.

the singers were upset that Britten and Pears and the opera's producer, Eric Crozier, were conscientious objectors. Clearly, the climate at Sadler's Wells was not conducive to further projects.

But Britten was already looking further afield. He had announced to Hawkes before starting to compose *Grimes* that he intended to 'write a few [operas] in my time', and that this might mean 'cutting down means a bit' (*LL2* 1128–9). Barely two months after *Grimes's* premiere he was writing to Pears with the news that plans were proceeding for their own opera company, which was to be based at Dartington Hall in Devon (1273). The intention was to focus, initially at least, on chamber opera, to be performed by a company of singers and instrumentalists handpicked by Britten and his close associates. In the event the Dartington venture fell through, but the notion of a new company survived, and the first opera written for it, *The Rape of Lucretia*, Op. 37, was produced in 1946 at Glyndebourne, a small opera house built by John Christie in 1934 in the grounds of his home. Britten's second chamber opera, *Albert Herring*, Op. 39, followed in 1947 – by which point the company had parted from Christie (due to tensions over a loss-making tour of *Lucretia*) and had been formalized as the English Opera Group.

Domesticity

In the wake of *Peter Grimes*, the patterns of domestic and professional life that were to underpin the rest of Britten's life emerged rapidly. As Paul Kildea observed, *Grimes's* success 'cemented the rehabilitation process' with the BBC,[24] and Britten's publisher's growing confidence in his commercial viability, influenced by the BBC's more agreeable stance, led to their offering him an increased retainer (of £600 pa) – which Britten promptly declined, telling Ralph Hawkes he was 'old-fashioned enough not to feel easy about receiving more than I actually earn' (*LL2* 1286). As a performer, too, his star was firmly in the ascendant, with enquiries coming in from around Europe.[25] After having had to grasp every opportunity for work – composition and performance – that came his way, Britten was now in a position to plan and control his workflow to a far greater extent. His personal life also was now more settled than at any time since his days in 'Heaven'. From this point on it is possible, at the risk of being overly reductive, to chart Britten's life in terms of two apparently opposing forces. There was an impulse towards domesticity: from the second half of 1945 Britten began to build up an extended form of the 'warm nest of love' of which Auden spoke (its 'stifling' effects would become an issue in the 1950s, and particularly pressing in the decade after). And yet there was also the pursuit of an increasing role as a public, even Establishment,

[24] *SB* 70.
[25] See *LL3* 145.

8. *Britten on the ski slopes in Switzerland, in 1947.*

figure. Philip Brett goes so far as to refer to his 'institutionalization' in the early 1960s.[26]

Britten's domestic life revolved, of course, around his relationship with Pears. Auden had described them, during their time in the US, as a married couple, and in a lot of ways they seem to have operated on this basis, negotiating with various degrees of success the tensions arising from competing professional demands and personal needs. Pears acquired a house in London in 1946, which Britten also used as his base in the capital (the couple shared it with six other people including Pears's parents).[27] Pears was always going to require London accommodation, and probably felt the need to assert and maintain a separate identity for the outside world; certainly the view of Isador Caplan, Britten's solicitor who arranged the purchase of the lease, was that Pears 'was very much a London man ... whereas Ben was happiest in Aldeburgh'.[28] However, Pears gave up the house when Britten moved in August 1947 from the Old Mill in Snape to Crag House on Aldeburgh's seafront, and for their

---

[26] *BBGO.*
[27] Christopher Headington, *Peter Pears: A Biography* (London: Faber & Faber, 1992), 138. See also *LL3* 191, note 25.
[28] *BB* 260.

London base the couple now rented rooms from Erwin Stein, Britten's editor at Boosey & Hawkes. Britten explained the move from the Mill in one of his catch-up letters to Elizabeth Mayer: 'I had in a way outgrown the Mill. I still have it – friends from Switzerland have rented it – but I wanted something simpler, bigger, & above all in front of the sea as before!' (LL3 357), 'as before' referring, clearly, to his Lowestoft childhood. He effected a reconstruction of 'Heaven' by having his studio on the first floor, looking out over the beach. But as his public profile increased and the whereabouts of the house became well known (passers-by would apparently stop and watch him at work), the idyll began to crumble. In November 1957 the couple moved to the greater privacy of the Red House on the outskirts of the town.

During both the Crag House and Red House occupancies the Britten–Pears household often extended to guests collaborating on operas or performance projects. Indeed it is easy to regard Britten's various concerns as the outgrowth or extension of domesticity: the English Opera Group, for example, may have been a rigorously professional activity, but the staff's devotedness to Britten, and the scale of the enterprise, suggests an extended-family mindset.[29] As had always been the case, Britten had someone to cook and keep house for him, and his personal staff later increased to include a secretary/driver (Jeremy Cullum) and, from September 1952, Imogen Holst as his amanuensis. His dislike of conducting orchestras with which he did not already have a working relationship further suggests a family mentality. The pragmatic reason for all this is obvious: if Britten were to fulfil his ambitions, he would need a comprehensive support system. And given that the true nature of his relationship with Pears was impossible to hide from those who worked closely with them, he probably felt it necessary to foster a close-knit community which he could trust.

There was once a genuine threat to his liberty. In December 1953 he was interviewed by Scotland Yard in connection with the anti-homosexuality campaign instigated by the Home Secretary, Sir David Maxwell-Fyfe, and in the summer of 1955 Sir Steuart Wilson, who had just stepped down as Deputy General Administrator of the Royal Opera House (and was in fact a distant relative of Pears), announced 'a campaign against homosexuality in British music'.[30] With this in the air, it would hardly have been surprising if Britten – who by then had had two new operas performed at Covent Garden, in 1951 and 1953 – felt the need to distance himself from institutions over which he had little influence, to close ranks, and form his own operation.

It is a plausible argument that Grimes's underlying compulsion is to achieve domestic stability and, through that, the utopia of the respectability

---

[29] This was also the case with the Aldeburgh Festival.
[30] See Donald Mitchell's introductory essay to LL3, 7.

he craves ('I'll marry Ellen'). Many of the operas Britten completed in the period after *Grimes* reverse this dynamic and present ordinary, even humdrum, domestic settings, or domestic elements, which are disturbed or put out of kilter in some way. This is most obviously the case in *The Rape of Lucretia*, in which idyllic domesticity and an ideal relationship are brutally ruptured by rape; despite the political backdrop (Tarquinius as invading Etruscan, and so on), and the wider implications that the Christian frame seeks to impose, this is a domestic crime, and all the more appalling for that. In *Albert Herring* the eponymous hero rebels against a suffocating domestic situation, while *The Turn of the Screw* revolves around the corruption of the settled, comfortable (and comforting) routine of a country house. In this context might also be mentioned Britten's setting of the Chester Miracle Play, *Noye's Fludde*, which, for all the symbolism and mythology, involves a single family (with the use of hymns extending the family circle beyond the performers to include the audience) – though the 'disturbance' here is obviously of a different kind. The domestic situation is an experience common to most human beings; it certainly was to Britten's audience, on whose imaginations the disturbances were likely to have had a strong impact.

Institutions new and old

The manifesto for the English Opera Group (EOG) was issued in the form of a four-page leaflet early in 1947. The key paragraphs regarding its intent are the first two:

> We believe the time has come when England, which has never had a tradition of native opera, but has always depended on a repertory of foreign works, can create its own operas. Opera is as much a vital means of artistic expression as orchestral music, drama, and painting. The lack of it has meant a certain impoverishment of English artistic life.
>
> We believe the best way to achieve the beginning of a repertory of English operas is through the creation of a form of opera requiring small resources of singers and players, but suitable for performance in large or small opera houses or theatres.[31]

The EOG's purpose and modus operandi were further expounded by Britten in a meeting on 5 April 1950 of the Arts Council of Great Britain Opera and Ballet Sub-Committee, a meeting which was convened to consult with the composer.[32] The document demonstrates very clearly Britten's practical approach, and the degree to which the sub-committee needed educating. (It also vividly demonstrates his sharpness of mind and sardonic wit.) Britten made the point that, as part of the process of

---

[31] Reproduced in *LL3* 243–4.
[32] A transcription is reproduced in *BoM* 86–101.

kick-starting a 'native tradition', younger singers would need to perform the same part many times in order to build up experience. And performing the same opera several times would give composers 'a chance to see where the mistakes in their works lie, what things are good and what things are bad, and to profit from that knowledge' (*BoM* 87). He signalled too the importance of touring, given that a smaller organization would not be able to sustain a large repertory 'which would enable us to stay in one place' (90); touring would also spread the risk of audience reaction to new work, which would inevitably vary from place to place.

Britten's interest in less-than-Grand opera would be sustained by the creation of the Aldeburgh Festival, in 1948, and for the cramped space of the Jubilee Hall (nevertheless the largest in town) he wrote, in the remarkably short space of seven months, *A Midsummer Night's Dream*, Op. 64 (1960). This was his first opera specifically for the Festival, and surprisingly so, since it was composed more than a decade after the Festival's founding – this is all the more striking given that the Festival 'was started by the [English Opera] Group and run entirely by it' (*BoM* 92). *A Midsummer Night's Dream* boasts a bigger cast and orchestra than his three other chamber operas (four, if his realization of *The Beggar's Opera* of 1948 is included), but the ensemble is still within chamber dimensions: flutes, clarinets and horns doubled, 4.2.2.2.2. strings, and percussion. Performance in a smallish theatre is needed if the audience is to be drawn into the opera's magical world.

In the 1960s the Festival environment would spawn a new type of chamber opera, the Church Parable, which employed even more slender resources. And at the end of that decade, with *Owen Wingrave*, Britten was writing opera for the smallest auditorium of all, the ordinary living room, through the medium of television; a work about the shattering of domestic life is thereby experienced in a domestic situation.

After the success of *Peter Grimes*, though, it is hardly surprising that Britten wished again to exploit the resources of the largest companies and houses, especially if he could secure a degree of control over casting and production (if less over the scheduling and general administration): some themes need the larger cast, stage, and orchestral canvas for their realization, and no opera composer of ambition can resist this for long. Thus in February 1947 – contemporaneously, in fact, with the hatching of the EOG – Crozier was reporting to the mezzo-soprano Nancy Evans that some of the people at the core of the EOG (Britten, Pears, Crozier himself, and John Piper) were hatching plans for an opera for Covent Garden on Cromwell and the Civil War – something which could hardly fit into a chamber format.[33] This idea was soon aborted, but the early 1950s did see Britten composing the two largest of his operatic scores in the span of just over three years.

---

[33] See *LL3* 288.

The first of these was *Billy Budd*, Op. 50 (1951), which Britten originally intended for Sadler's Wells to premiere at the 1951 Edinburgh Festival, though the work was eventually commissioned by the Arts Council for performance at Covent Garden during the 1951 Festival of Britain after Sadler's Wells's arrangements fell through.[34] As far back as 1946 Britten had written to Hawkes that he was enthusiastic about composing an opera for Covent Garden, but that when it came to terms 'it must be clear that I have the veto on performers & producer & conductor. I have no faith in an organisation which has [Constant] Lambert as assistant conductor, & on the Committee behind it – Walton & Dent' (*LL3* 199). Britten's desire for control is noteworthy; no doubt, in his own mind, this was not simply for itself but to ensure the highest standards. In 1948 his doubts about the Royal Opera's abilities were still entrenched: in May he wrote to David Webster, General Administrator of the Royal Opera House, that he was shocked by the standard of a performance of *Grimes* that he'd seen there, pointing to under-rehearsal and miscasting as two central problems;[35] while in October, in response to Webster's initial request that he provide a work for the 1951 Festival of Britain, Britten asserted that before making any commitment he would have to be 'very strongly assured that my demands will be met'. The letter ended with 'best wishes to you all in spite of our differences' (437).

Clearly, though, the climate had changed by August 1950. Britten and Webster had met to talk about a possible operatic or cinematic adaptation of *The Tempest* with John Gielgud (another aborted project) and Britten wrote afterwards: 'I enjoyed my talk with you. You were very accommodating … & I feel we can now go forward on a fine footing' (*LL3* 602). And by December of that year Britten was writing to the co-librettist of *Budd*, E. M. Forster, of an improved relationship with the Royal Opera House.[36] However, the relationship would again come under considerable strain during the production of Britten's next opera, *Gloriana*, Op. 53, which was performed in the presence of Queen Elizabeth II during her Coronation Gala. Only seven days before its first performance on 8 June 1953 Britten was writing furiously to Webster after confusion over providing a fanfare for the royal party's arrival led to the General Administrator asking Britten to do it at the last moment. Britten said it was exactly what he thought would happen:

> It comes, I fear, like so many things at the Opera House, from your not making up your mind in time, or if you have decided something imagining that other people are thought-readers. Often people help you out at considerable wear & strain to themselves, but this time I cannot help you … Perhaps if the musical side of the House were

---

[34] *LL3* 436–8 and 563–7.
[35] See *LL3* 436–7.
[36] *LL3* 632.

better organized I might be able to – but the wear of these last weeks, coping with hopeless arrangements has been too great. Besides <u>IT IS TOO LATE</u> … And don't, David, go round saying I've let you down, because it isn't true. (*LL4* 144–5)[37]

There were also jealousies to contend with. The Royal Ballet were miffed because they weren't involved in the Gala, which led to attempts to stage a ballet before the opera – upon which Britten stomped: 'only over my dead body, & dead opera too, will there be a ballet before *Gloriana* that night' (*LL4* 97). Walton was piqued too, writing to the librettist of his own opera, *Troilus and Cressida* (a project he interrupted to work on music for the Coronation service itself): 'Owing to Harewood's royal connections he has wangled that the Queen has commanded an opera for the Coronation season. It is, I need hardly say, not T&C, but a new one "Elizabeth & Essex" by Billy Britten … we've no friends at Court so we must put on a smiling face and pretend we like it' (107).

'Harewood' was Earl Harewood, first cousin of the Queen. He had married Marion Stein, daughter of Erwin Stein, in 1949. *Billy Budd* was dedicated to the couple. They hosted a dinner party at their London home for the Queen and Prince Philip to preview extracts from *Gloriana*, sung by Pears and Joan Cross with Britten at the piano. Harewood reports in his memoirs that Britten was only interested in the project if it were 'made in some way official, not quite commanded but at least accepted as part of the celebrations' (*LL4* 58), and the appeal of official patronage is clear: securing the top musical event of the Coronation celebrations would confer in many people's eyes Britten's status as the nation's premier composer. But it would be unjustified to conclude that he was entirely comfortable with being associated with the court. He later refused a knighthood, for instance,[38] and his statement that receiving the Companion of Honour in the Coronation honours list was 'a compliment to serious English music & what is more – opera' (163) seems entirely genuine in its deflection. He had further contact with the monarchy later in life: he had lunch with the Queen in 1957, and ten years later invited her to open the Maltings concert hall at Snape; the Queen commissioned *A Birthday Hansel* for tenor and harp for her mother's seventy-fifth birthday in 1975. There appears to have been a genuinely warm regard for Britten on the part of both royal personages, and this seems to have been reciprocated.[39] Britten developed friendships with other royals and aristocrats, too, including Prince Ludwig of Hesse and the Rhine and his

---

[37] Britten was not the only composer to be frustrated by Webster. In March/April 1954 Michael Tippett wrote to his publishers, Schott: 'so far as can ever be with [Webster], the meeting was satisfactory … He is himself excessively dilatory and so everything gets left till too late.' *Selected Letters of Michael Tippett*, ed. Thomas Schuttenhelm (London: Faber & Faber, 2005), 43.

[38] *BB* 579.

[39] John Bridcut, *The Faber Pocket Guide to Britten* (London: Faber & Faber, 2010), 157–70.

wife Princess Margaret, to whom he was introduced by Harewood in 1952.[40] It was to them that he wrote some appreciative words about Prince Philip after meeting him in their home in 1958: 'It was very nice to meet the D. of Edinb. I had found it hard to believe what you & Peg had always said, that he was nice, sympathetic & intelligent – but my goodness, he really is' (LL5 22). And yet, in a letter to Pears in 1963, he was comparing the Hesses, favourably, to 'all these other dreary HRH's, you know – these hopeless misfits who go around condemning everything new in their snobbish way' (482). Replying to this, Pears mused that he and Britten were hardly royalty-friendly: 'we are after all queer & left & conshies which is enough to put us, or make us put ourselves, outside the pale.'[41]

From the perspective of audience reception, the first performance of *Gloriana* was a disaster. Replying to one of Harewood's friends who hadn't been present, Britten wrote: 'You didn't miss much on Monday night because the Gala was a shocking occasion – an audience of stuck pigs – but I hope you'll see her later under more auspicious circumstances' (LL4 147). Harewood himself recalled that 'The audience, so far from being a gathering of artistic Britain to honour the Queen (as we had naively hoped), consisted of Cabinet, Diplomatic Corps and official London first and foremost, and the rest apparently nowhere.'[42] It does seem naive to have expected that the audience would be anything other than what it was, and odd that no one associated with Britten was able to predict that a story that ended with the ageing Elizabeth I standing on stage without her wig moments before her death would not go down well. As with *Our Hunting Fathers*, Britten had delivered what can only be viewed as an inappropriate work for the occasion, however impressive the musical result. Perhaps he had had his eye on the work's subsequent performances in front of his 'normal' audience, the audience that had responded enthusiastically to *Budd*. These later performances were rather more successful, though not as successful as Britten suggested in some of his letters to friends: in *Gloriana*'s re-run in January and February 1954, audiences averaged only thirty-six per cent.[43]

The experience of *Gloriana*'s first night led to Pears, who was unhappy about his role in the production and had threatened to pull out, to wonder whether future operas should be aimed squarely at Aldeburgh audiences whose support had already been gained.[44] In essence, this is what happened: while Britten's operas continued to be revived at Covent Garden, or, in the case of new ones, were transferred there, they were never again composed specifically for it. During the composition of

---

[40] LL4 200, note 3.
[41] BB 419.
[42] From his memoir *The Tongs and the Bones*, quoted in LL4 150.
[43] SB 143.
[44] LL4 150.

Gloriana Britten was in fact offered the post of music director, with Webster suggesting that he had a duty to English music to undertake it.[45] Britten quickly declined. He did, however, get drawn into the House again in 1956, composing for them his only published ballet, *The Prince of the Pagodas*, Op. 57, with John Cranko as choreographer. The project was again full of problems, some of which can only be laid at the composer's door – such as his misjudgement of the time and energy required to complete the score in the middle of a schedule that was already punishing. There were the usual communication difficulties with Webster, too. Composition was interrupted by Britten's five-month trip through Europe and India to the Far East (a tour which would be of the greatest significance for his compositional development), and the ballet was postponed. While this eased some of the tension, the Royal Opera House failed to find a major conductor to take it on and Britten had to conduct the first three performances before retiring to Aldeburgh to rest on doctor's orders.

The Aldeburgh Festival was not without its squalls, either. A number of entries in Imogen Holst's diary record Britten's exasperation after Festival Committee Meetings. In one meeting of 1952 he tried to steer through plans to increase the seating capacity of the Jubilee Hall, after which he was 'so depressed … that he couldn't work the following day'.[46] By this date the Festival had expanded and was becoming a major national, if not international, event. Its origins had been rather more homely: Pears had come up with the idea for the Festival while driving to Lucerne with Britten and Crozier for EOG performances of *Herring* and *Lucretia*.[47] Plans were put in place for the 1948 Festival on their return, with a meeting being called to rouse local support. The Festival, which was essentially run by the EOG, was to include – as well as musical performances – talks about the other arts and exhibitions of paintings or sculpture. The initial venues were the Jubilee Hall and the local church. The inaugural Festival included a performance of *Albert Herring* and the first performance of the cantata *Saint Nicolas*, Op. 42, which had been composed for the centenary celebrations of Pears's old school, Lancing College, where the official premiere took place three weeks later. With its mixture of professional and amateur forces (the former including Pears singing the title role, the latter the orchestra and the Festival choir), and a prominent role for the audience (who join in the singing of the hymns that mark the end of each part), *Saint Nicolas* was a propitious piece with which to establish the Festival 'ethos' and to actualize Britten's ideal of the composer serving the community.

---

[45] Reported in Imogen Holst's diaries in Christopher Grogan (ed.), *Imogen Holst: A Life in Music* (Woodbridge: Boydell Press, 2007), 169.

[46] Ibid., 151.

[47] Judith LeGrove, 'Aldeburgh', in Mervyn Cooke (ed.), *The Cambridge Companion to Benjamin Britten* (Cambridge: Cambridge University Press, 1999), 306.

9. *Going for a spin: Britten and the children of the original cast of his 'entertainment for young people',* Let's Make an Opera, *set off in his Rolls (June 1949).*

Britten's Festival roles included that of artistic director (an unofficial title at first, becoming official, and shared with Pears, from 1955; other directors – Imogen Holst and Philip Ledger – came later), accompanist, conductor and, of course, composer-in-residence. The programming included works Britten thought neglected and needed airing: the Festival was the launchpad for his rehabilitation of Bridge, for example. The Festival later expanded to include prominent guest artists from overseas (Rostropovich, Richter), and visiting major composers such as Copland, Henze, Kodály, Lutosławski, Poulenc and Shostakovich. And as the number of events grew, so did the venues (with the churches at Blythburgh and Orford, and Snape Maltings being enlisted). Britten might not have needed the Festival as an outlet for his music, and might have been better off without the organizational encumbrance, but it did afford him control over performance conditions that he wouldn't have obtained elsewhere, and ensured the reception of new works by a core of devotees.

It was perhaps inevitable, as the Festival grew in size, ambition and reputation, that Britten would become distant from many of the people at the 'coalface', administrators and musicians alike. Some felt that the 'family' atmosphere gave way, in the EOG as well as in the Festival, to something more 'them-and-us': one of the people Carpenter interviewed said that they called Britten's inner circle 'the Royal Family'.[48] The change in atmosphere seems to have happened in around 1953. Perhaps Britten was drawing into himself a little more as the result of the pressures of *Gloriana*. Certainly there are signs in the 1950s of him beginning to find his work schedule difficult to cope with, and his various bouts of illness may well have resulted from this. It has been suggested that the gathering (consciously or not) of an inner circle around him could have been a way of supporting himself through all the pressures. Delegation was a necessary consequence of how he felt he had to work. This led, though, to sometimes shockingly insensitive handling of dismissals, which Britten frequently left to others.[49]

New lines

Three months after the premiere of *Grimes* Britten completed his String Quartet No. 2, Op. 36. He wrote to Mary Behrend, the dedicatee: 'I am so glad you got pleasure from it because to my mind it is the greatest advance that I have yet made, & altho' it is far from perfect, it has given me encouragement to continue on new lines' (*LL2* 1285). While one might form the impression that, beginning with *Grimes*, it is opera in which Britten's most important musical achievements and developments (or 'advancements') are to be found, this was not indubitably the case as far as the composer was concerned. The list of non-operatic works including the *Spring Symphony*, Op. 44 and the various Canticles and song-cycles would tend to support him. Britten might well have been inflating the quartet's significance in order to ingratiate himself with the dedicatee, but there seems no need for him to do this. He went on to say, 'People don't understand it as they do the Donne [song-cycle *Holy Sonnets of John Donne*, Op. 35 for tenor and piano], but that is because those wonderful words help so.'

Identifying exactly what Britten meant in his letter by 'new lines' is not easy, for there are no obvious technical changes in the quartet, as there were in his music of later in the decade. He might simply be referring to the influence of Purcell: the three-movement quartet ends with one of Purcell's favourite forms, the passacaglia (a set of variations over a repeated bass, though the bass line can – and in Britten's case does – occasionally migrate to higher parts of the texture), as, indeed, does the Donne song-cycle. Or he might have meant a greater 'purity', or seriousness, of style – in that 'characteristic' music, or parody as employed in *Grimes*, is eschewed. However, the 'characteristic' approach is certainly

---

[48] *BB* 319.
[49] Various cases are detailed in *BB*: see, for example, 319ff.

apparent in another Purcell-influenced work from 1945, the famous *Young Person's Guide to the Orchestra*, Op. 34, completed in December despite the earlier opus number, and subtitled 'variations and fugue on a theme of Henry Purcell'. Britten would continue to refer to other music for either comedic or ironic effect (as in, respectively, *Albert Herring* and *The Turn of the Screw*), but after *Grimes* he generally relied much less on effects resulting from the manipulation of stylistic models.

The reduced dimensions of *The Rape of Lucretia* do not appear to have led to a wholesale rethinking of Britten's operatic practice, but they did lead, inevitably, to his consideration of the most effective use of much smaller vocal and instrumental resources. The opera's compositional circumstances tended to reinforce the 'less-is-more' tenet central to Britten's aesthetics: it is a fully-fledged drama involving complex issues fashioned from relatively slender means. One way of creating a sense of 'big drama' is to situate the action within a wider context, and this may have been one of Britten's

10. *An early rehearsal for the first performances of* The Rape of Lucretia *at Glyndebourne in 1946; Ernest Ansermet is conducting, with Britten at the piano.*

motivations for the use of the tenor and soprano solos that act as the Greek chorus, setting up (and later commenting upon) the historical and political contexts; the opening recitative for the Male Chorus, for instance, launches the work with the bald historical fact that 'Rome is now ruled by the Etruscan upstart: Tarquinius Superbus'.[50]

In contrast with the operas composed either side of it, *Lucretia* is generally static in terms of what we see on the stage, which makes the violence of the rape itself and Lucretia's suicide all the more harrowing. Dramatic tension is skilfully controlled. A good example of this can be seen in Act I, after the initial scene-setting from the Male Prologue. The curtain rises on 'a camp outside Rome, with the Generals' tent in foreground'. Britten weaves a nocturnal backcloth of gently undulating chords (muted strings) whose mild dissonance is always just out of reach of full resolution – a vivid evocation of sultriness ('the air / Sits on their backs like a heavy bear'). At the top and bottom of the texture, harp oscillations and plucked double-bass glissandos serve as cricket and bullfrog sounds respectively (Britten here sails very close to the wind in terms of the obviousness of his musical illustration, but gets away with it because of the sophistication of the overall context). Against this the Male Chorus describes the brooding atmosphere. He is interrupted twice by the Generals' vigorous exhortations of the pleasure of wine, which, tailing off rather than effecting genuine harmonic progression, emphasizes, rather than lightens, the melancholy.

The language of the Male Chorus here is distinctly on the purple side, and the libretto has been much criticized for being excessively and self-consciously literary. The librettist, Ronald Duncan, observed excesses himself, asking Britten some years after the first production if he could see his way to revising the line, uttered on the third page of the vocal score, 'With the prodigious liberality / Of self-coin'd obsequious flattery'. Britten politely declined: 'I will discuss with Peter [Pears, for whom the Male Chorus was written] about the "prodigious liberality etc." – but I've got rather fond of it, & he does it very convincingly!' (*LL3* 258). This is not the worst example, though: candidates for this prize might be the Female Chorus's 'The oatmeal slippers of sleep / Creep through the city and drag / The sable shadows of night / Over the limbs of light', or Tarquinius' observation of Lucretia sleeping: 'Loveliness like this is never chaste; / If not enjoyed it is just waste.' Duncan had helped out with the odd corner of the *Grimes* libretto behind Montagu Slater's back when Britten was dissatisfied with the latter's efforts, but Duncan was soon likewise to find himself unwanted: he had been busy reworking Jane Austen's *Mansfield Park* as Britten's proposed next opera for Glyndebourne when Marion Stein

---

[50] The stage action is further contextualized by the Chorus's obviously temporally dislocated Christian deliberations. The reader is directed to Peter Evans, *The Music of Benjamin Britten* (2nd edn, London: Dent, 1989), 141–3, for a succinct identification and discussion of the problems.

told him the composer was now working on *Albert Herring* with Crozier.[51] While Britten was able to reconcile himself with the libretto of *Lucretia* (though it still seems remarkable that he didn't demand a reworking of some of its excesses), he also saw that, if its language could be held appropriate for that particular project, as a general working principle he needed texts that were less overwrought.

Despite its problems, *Lucretia* contains some of Britten's finest and most characteristic music. As Peter Evans points out, 'No commentator seems able to withhold a reference to the scoring of Lucretia's sleep music,'[52] which has a prominent role for alto flute and bass clarinet. The overall effect owes as much, though, to the gently luminous diatonic dissonances that also characterize the women's spinning music and the 'Goodnight' chorus. All of these are troubled idylls, and all suggest – like 'From the gutter' – an empathy with women that is generally overlooked in studies of the composer.

Not the least importance of *Lucretia*, so far as Britten was concerned, lay in the number of performances the work received. In his 1950 meeting with the Arts Council sub-committee he had noted that, while *Grimes* received twelve performances in its first season, *Lucretia* had one hundred during its first two seasons, enabling him (he claimed) to be more aware of the mistakes and develop more certainly as a result. Whether or not this can be classified as one of the mistakes, it is noticeable that *Lucretia* sketches the psychological motivations of several characters, while *Grimes* is the psychological portrait chiefly of one character. And *Albert Herring* returns to revolving around one character – though we don't get inside Albert's mind in the same way as we get inside Grimes's: or, at least, not so obviously and dramatically.

Albert Herring is Britten's social comedy, less disturbing than *Grimes* but arguably more subversive. In it he gives his skill at parody full rein: for example, most of the music for the village worthies is based on pre-existent types of one kind or another, worked so as to lay bare the characters' limited horizons and pomposity. However, the most significant (and most famous) reference to 'other music' in *Herring* is not parody as such, but a literal quotation of the 'Tristan' chord at the moment Albert celebrates his being crowned King of the May by drinking the lemonade that Sid has secretly laced with rum. The chord is often seen as a symbol of longing (it demands resolution and explanation, engendering in the rest of Wagner's opera a chromatic style replete with yearning), but it also symbolizes liberation, of a sort, in its association with the love-potion that Brangena slips into Tristan's and Isolde's drinks, compelling them to ignore the restraints imposed by their social and political circumstances and fall in

---

[51] See *LL3* 232.
[52] Evans, *The Music of Benjamin Britten*, 126.

love. Albert is in desperate need of liberation, too, and his libation opens the door to a night of self-discovery. Michael Wilcox has drawn attention to various 'markers' that support the case for the story being of one individual's recognition and acceptance of his homosexuality. The chapter in which Wilcox does this is called 'Albert comes out',[53] but Albert doesn't come out, of course (it is 1947), and the opera ends with studied musical conventionality – exactly the kind of rousing cadence one would expect to round off a comedy. Arnold Whittall commented that 'Albert seems content for the moment to exercise his maturity within a familiar society rather than beyond it',[54] a position that Britten's compositional stance (with its intent to create new, often subversive, contexts employing old materials and procedures) seems ideal to portray. The resonances with Britten's own life in the late 1940s do not need to be laboured.

It could be said that all opera composition is about learning how to make positive use of the genre's peculiar restrictions. Britten's chamber operas show the extent to which he revelled in this, and he was obviously highly stimulated by stage and musical problem-solving. In returning to the larger stage with *Billy Budd* he naturally had bigger resources at his disposal, but had to cope with two major restrictions: the necessity for an all-male cast (there being no women aboard a late-eighteenth-century British man-of-war), and the action taking place at sea in close confines. The latter was solved by clever set design; the former would only truly be problematic for a composer lacking ability in characterization, into which category Britten manifestly didn't fall.

In the early stages of composing the opera Britten had written to Hawkes: 'As usual I am afraid the subject and the treatment will be controversial, but I know you are used to that!' (*LL3* 501). He might have been referring to the all-male cast, but was more likely thinking of the homo-erotic overtones that the majority of recent commentators have identified. Without being aware of these it is perfectly possible to read the story simply as a tragedy of a charismatic and naively goodhearted sailor who, unable to articulate his rage in any other way, lashes out at and kills his unjust accuser (the master-at-arms, Claggart); he is condemned to death, yet forgives the captain, Vere, who instigates the trial with needless haste without giving rein to possible alternatives. Vere seems remorseful when he looks back over events in the Epilogue: 'But he has saved me and blessed me, and the love that passes understanding has come to me.' The biblical reference suggests this 'love' is of the platonic, Christian variety. But such is the force of Claggart's animosity towards Billy (far more passionate than would be suggested by a simple envy of Billy's beauty,

---

[53] Wilcox, *Benjamin Britten's Operas*, 37–44.
[54] Arnold Whittall, 'The Chamber Operas', in Cooke (ed.), *The Cambridge Companion to Benjamin Britten*, 103–4.

handsomeness and goodness – of which he sings in his vindictive aria) that a deeply buried, repressed force seems the only adequate explanation. The central relationship, though, is that between Billy and Vere, and it is this that in Philip Brett's view gave Forster in his libretto the chance 'symbolically to evoke the power of homosexual love without being in any way sexually explicit'.[55]

If the type of love of which Vere speaks is ambiguous, it is one ambiguity of many in *Billy Budd*. Perhaps the main one is what the opera is essentially about. According to Arnold Whittall, 'it is the inevitable triumph of doubt over certainty that is the "moral", not the simple banishment of guilt through forgiveness.'[56] Nowhere is this more powerfully expressed than in the climax of the Epilogue, the massive B flat major chord that is the final harmonic event of the work. It is one of the most remarkable moments in all of Britten's output. Such an overwhelming effect of, simultaneously, utter triumph and devastating deadness can only be created by a composer at the height of his powers. The triumph is conveyed partly through gesture (a big, loud, *tutti* chord), and partly through the apparently decisive resolution of the conflict with which the opera began and which is reinvoked at the opening of the Epilogue: a dichotomy between B flat major and B minor (a particularly biting semitone clash). The deadness is the consequence of events in the preceding scene, in which Billy, as the stage directions direct, 'ascends the mast' to be hanged and 'the crew on the main deck turns in rebellion to the quarter deck'. At this point the crew sing a highly agitated, fugue-like texture rising in register and volume as they become more threatening. This music at its peak coalesces into the B minor chord, but by this stage the officers have begun barking 'Down all hands' on a conflicting B flat, reaching their own peak of volume at the same time as the crew (and, unlike the crew, they have the heavy orchestral brass to back them up). From here the crew's music gradually yields and folds itself into the B flat layer. It is because B flat-Authority has simply asserted itself with brute force that the 'triumphant' chord in the Epilogue seems so false. The falsity is reaffirmed almost as soon as the chord is sounded: very soon it begins to fade. No one listening to Vere's music – as distinct from his words – during his final reflection can find his view of events convincing; his final bars of recitative conflict with the dying-away B flat chord, apart from the note D, his final note, which, in being the element in common between the B flat and B minor triads, is suffused with ambiguity. The effect is summed up by Whittall:

> the nature of the final resolution onto a pure B flat major is such that it is possible to regard the actual elimination of dissonance, when

---

[55] Philip Brett, 'Salvation at Sea: Britten's *Billy Budd*', in Brett, *Music and Sexuality in Britten*, 72.
[56] Arnold Whittall, '"Twisted Relations": Method and Meaning in Britten's "Billy Budd"', *Cambridge Opera Journal*, 2/2 (1990), 171.

achieved, as a distinctly hollow triumph – not least because Vere's concluding phrases do not simply conform to it, but reinforce the impression of Vere as an archetypal Ancient Mariner, or even like the Flying Dutchman, unable to die and forced to relive the experiences he recounts in a hellish kind of endless present.[57]

This lengthy description has been given in order to indicate the skill with which Britten rethinks the role of thoroughly traditional elements of music – in this case the triad or common chord. The use of the triad that is most celebrated in commentaries on the opera is, however, in the interlude between scenes 2 and 3 of Act II – a kind of musical curtain which obscures the meeting between Billy and Vere before the former's execution. The musical substance here is a succession of triads that at first are not related in any traditional way, their non-relatedness emphasized by contrasts in instrumentation and dynamic. Gradually the harmony begins to crystallize around the tonic and dominant of F major, the whole sequence representing, perhaps, Billy's move towards acceptance of his fate – though it is of the essence that we do not know exactly what passes between him and Vere. Vere enters the state-room to tell Billy his fate full of uncertainty: 'I am the messenger of death, the messenger of death! How can he pardon? How receive me?'

Gloriana also contains a trial, and the condemning of a man to death (the Earl of Essex), about which the other central character (the eponymous Elizabeth I) is again conflicted. But in most ways this is a very different opera to *Budd*. As inventive in its orchestration as any Britten score, and fascinating in its evocation of public and private worlds, it is less overtly dramatic in stage presentation than his previous operas, ending with a distillation of Elizabeth's melancholy majesty before her quiet death.

'On the threshold of a new musical world'

After completing *Gloriana* Britten wrote another letter in which he indicated a change of direction. This time the correspondent was Edith Sitwell, whose poem 'Still Falls the Rain' he had set in his *Canticle III: Still Falls the Rain*, Op. 55 for tenor, horn and piano. He says:

I feel with this work & the Turn of the Screw ... that I am on the threshold of a new musical world (for me, I am not pretentious about it!). I am worried by the problems which arise, & that is one reason that I am taking off next winter to do some deep thinking. But your great poem has dragged something from me that was latent there, & shown me what lies before me. (*LL4* 316)

Here it is a little clearer what Britten is talking about than in the letter to Mary Behrend which mentions 'new lines'. Both *Canticle III* and *The Turn*

---

57 Ibid.

of the Screw make constructional use of what music theorists refer to as the twelve-tone aggregate – that is, the twelve notes in the chromatic scale conceived as a structural unit. While Britten took an interest in Schoenberg in the years just before and during his time at the RCM this interest seems to have been most in the Schoenberg who had jettisoned tonality but had not yet formalized the consequent atonality into the constructivist deployment of the twelve-tone aggregate known as twelve-tone serialism. In this method of composition the order of the notes of the aggregate – the 'series' (sometimes 'set' or 'row') – remains fixed; the series is manipulated in various ways (including mirror inversion and retrogression, as well as transposition) to produce all the pitch-material of the work: melody and, by 'verticalizing' adjacent notes of the series, harmony. Britten's music is never serial in the manner of Schoenberg's or Berg's, in which it is a fundamental structural element;[58] but the constructivist in him clearly found some, at least, of the principles appealing, and some of the associated techniques form an important part of his toolbox from this point on. Often the principle employed is one of completion, so that a structural unit might be defined by the unfolding of all twelve tones without order necessarily being of importance. It is this, along with the use of inversion (though this isn't just a trait of serialism), that characterizes the instrumental variations of *Canticle III*.

One of the central questions for composers for whom some kind of tonal structuring is fundamental but who wish to use aspects of twelve-tone procedures is how to reconcile the two, for they would appear to be incompatible. Another question has often been – and certainly was for Britten – the extent to which twelve-tone procedures can be apprehended and understood by listeners. In *The Turn of the Screw*, Op. 54 (1954), one of the works in which Britten's constructivist bent is most to the fore, the twelve-tone theme that is the basis for the opera gives prominence to the interval most associated with tonal progression, the fifth (and its inversion, the fourth).

As is customarily the case with Britten, the technical machinations serve dramatic and expressive ends. The composer himself noted parallels between the music's structural organization and the opera's plot line, which was adapted from Henry James's short story. He had been trying out various different titles for the work, and wrote to his librettist, Myfanwy Piper, during composition: 'I must confess I have a sneaking, horrid feeling that the original H.J. title describes the musical plan of the work <u>exactly</u>!!' (*LL4* 230). The key scheme certainly creates an almost unbearable culmination of tension, ending up with a head-on battle

---

[58] *Wozzeck*, Britten's favourite work by Berg, is atonal but non-serial; Berg's Violin Concerto – which also particularly impressed Britten – is serial, however, although of a kind that admits some of the traditional building-blocks of tonality, notably triads.

between two keys a semitone apart (A and A flat), while a strong sense of claustrophobia results from the 'closed' form (a series of variations, constantly reworking the same material), the dense motivic usage, and the almost exclusive use of the high voice range (Mrs Grose, a mezzo-soprano, is the only exception). One significant factor in establishing a sense of pervading vulnerability is the intimacy which the smallness of the instrumental ensemble creates; it draws the audience ineluctably into the increasingly fragile domestic world on the stage.

The main theme of the opera is generally held to be the corruption of innocence. It becomes apparent as the opera progresses that the children are being drawn into what the central protagonist, the Governess, sees as a web of depravity; and in the process of discovering this and trying to halt it she finds her own innocence shattered too. Yet ambiguities abound, not least in the precise location of the boundary between 'Good' and 'Evil'. It is never clear exactly what 'knowledge' Quint, the apparently deceased manservant, is bestowing upon Miles, the Governess's older charge (the assumption is likely to be that it is sexual, and James himself, when asked what interpretation should be placed upon the story, replied 'the worst possible'), but Britten ensures that the audience understands its allure for Miles and his sister, Flora. When Quint first establishes his presence and calls to Miles, we hear some of the most beguiling music to leave Britten's pencil, framed by the equally enticing sonority of the celesta. Miss Jessel, the Governess's predecessor, summons Flora in similarly exotic tones. And the richness of sonority is paralleled in the language both 'ghosts' employ, which includes a quotation from Yeats's 'The Second Coming' ('the ceremony of innocence is drowned'). Such is the bewitchment of this alternative world that one's discomfort on leaving the opera house is not so much at the chilling denouement – the death of Miles – as at having been seduced, even ravished, by that world, and being made complicit with what happens in it.

The beguiling sonorities may well have been prompted by Britten's second-hand contact with gamelan music via Colin McPhee's two-piano arrangements, which he played through during his sojourn in the US, and he probably also heard some of McPhee's tape recordings. First-hand experience came during what Britten referred to as his 'Great Tour', his trip to the Far East via Europe and India, which seems to have replaced the notion of 'taking off next winter to do some deep thinking' that Britten had mentioned to Edith Sitwell. He and Pears set off in October 1955, returning in March 1956.[59] As well as gamelan he heard Japanese Nō, Kabuki and Gagaku, which all made a great impact. To Imogen Holst

[59] This is documented in some detail in Mervyn Cooke, *Britten and the Far East* (Woodbridge: Boydell Press and The Britten-Pears Library, 1997), as well as in *LL4* (through his letters to Roger Duncan, which almost take the form of a travel diary), and in Philip Reed (ed.), *The Travel Diaries of Peter Pears 1936–1978* (Woodbridge: Boydell & Brewer, 1995).

he wrote from Bali: 'The music is <u>fantastically</u> rich – melodicly, rhythmicly, texture (such <u>orchestration</u>!!) & above all <u>formally</u>. It is a remarkable culture ... At last I'm beginning to catch on to the technique, but it's about as complicated as Schönberg' (*LL4* 385). About the Nō play that he saw in Tokyo he wrote to Roger Duncan:

> The Noh is very severe, classical – very traditional, without any scenery to speak of, or lighting and there are very few characters – one main one, who wears a mask, & two or three supporting ones & usually a very small boy too. There is a chorus that sits at the side, chanting, & a kind of orchestra of 2 drums (who also moan in the oddest way) & a flute, that squat in the centre of the stage, almost in the middle of the action. At first it all seemed too silly, & we giggled a lot. But soon we began to catch on a bit, & at the end it was very exciting. It's funny that if you are a good enough actor, just one movement suggests lots of things, & in the Noh, there are <u>very</u> few movements ... There was one called 'Sumida River' [*Sumidagawa*] which we saw twice. (*LL4* 409)

Britten notated parts of some of the various types of music that he heard, and arranged for recordings to be made.[60] His Far East experience had a profound effect on his musical 'language', though the most far-reaching effects were not felt until the mid-1960s. Not only did gamelan and Nō, in particular, help to reinvigorate his technique, they also provided potent symbols. It was gamelan that had the most immediate influence: Britten had left the UK in the middle of composing his ballet *Prince of the Pagodas*, and when he returned to the work he incorporated a virtual arrangement of the gamelan music he had had recorded on tape.

Gamelan sonorities do not have such an obvious presence in *A Midsummer Night's Dream*, but as in *The Turn of the Screw*, aspects of the sonorous conception – here, those associated with magic – could be seen as being derived from that world. And as with *The Turn of the Screw*, recent criticism has seen the 'exotic' elements as markers of homosexuality. Brett commented that 'If Quint is marked as homosexual and threateningly so by his "oriental" music, then Oberon is similarly designated by his countertenor voice; as Wayne Koestenbaum points out in a recent essay, the association of *falsetto* with unnaturalness and perversity in the singing manuals of the nineteenth century prefigures the discourse of homosexuality.'[61] Oberon's magical domain is further characterized by familiar aspects of Western music being 'made strange'. Hence the Wood music for strings moves through major triads on all twelve notes of the chromatic scale, and clear

---

[60] Excerpts can be found on the CD bundled with Cooke, *Britten and the Far East*.
[61] Philip Brett, 'Eros and Orientalism in Britten's Operas', in *Music and Sexuality in Britten*, 142. The Koestenbaum essay Brett refers to is 'The Queen's Throat: (Homo)sexuality and the Art of Singing', in Diana Fuss (ed.), *Inside/Out: Lesbian Theories, Gay Theories* (New York: Routledge, 1991), 217–23.

11. Stop-off on the world tour: Britten and Pears arrive by plane at Delhi, 28 December 1955.

harmonic orientation (the sense of being on stable ground) is further blurred by having the strings glissando between chords. In the Sleep music in Act II traditional chords (the notes of which again make up a twelve-tone aggregate) are subject to non-traditional juxtaposition. Meanwhile the strangeness of Oberon's offsider, or henchman, Puck comes from a kind of reversal of strangeness, for rather than sing (a strange thing to do in everyday social intercourse, after all, but conventional and expected in opera) he speaks only; perhaps to compensate, though, he is also required to perform acrobatics.

Inevitably, some commentators have seized upon the source of disagreement between Oberon and Tytania – which of them should have possession of an Indian changeling boy – and have related it to Britten's own obsession with boys. Wilcox complains that what happens to the boy is left unsaid, and is left entirely to the interpretation of directors.[62] But he fails to recognize that, for both Britten and Shakespeare (whose text the composer and Pears adapted as the libretto), the issue of the Indian boy is

[62] Wilcox, *Benjamin Britten's Operas*, 75–8.

essentially a MacGuffin – a device whose sole purpose is to set the plot in motion and is thereafter forgotten.

It is interesting to compare *A Midsummer Night's Dream* with Britten's only other operatic comedy, *Albert Herring*. The *Dream* too has moments of parody, but these are concentrated in the Mechanicals' play, which lampoons the conventions of nineteenth-century opera and features some enjoyable musical buffoonery. But a comparison of the serious, potentially allegorical aspects of the operas is most interesting. Both operas return to 'normality', or the so-called real world, after the transfiguring events set in train by mischief have run their course. In *Herring* the life of the central character is fundamentally transformed, even if he has to live that life under the cloak of conventionality; in the *Dream*, though, the endpoint is the restoration of what was erroneously changed. The substance of Britten's *Dream* (that is, Shakespeare's *Dream* transformed by his music) is not really the transformations themselves but the medium, the alternative reality, in which they take place. And for the audience the opera's substance could be said to be about music's power to enchant – particularly the kind of music that continues to find a place for traditional elements, the sort that Britten composed. In this way, and despite in many respects being untypical in terms of subject matter, *A Midsummer Night's Dream* fits into a larger 'Britten project' – conscientious service to society – that had been in train since his time at the RCM (if not before), but which he began to articulate publicly only in the 1960s.

Performing

Even in the twentieth century, when musical specialization – already well entrenched from the legacy of the nineteenth – reached its peak, it was common for composers to take to the concert platform or orchestra pit. To mention just a small sample of Britten's immediate predecessors and contemporaries: Stravinsky, Ravel, Bartók, Poulenc, Prokofiev, Shostakovich and Copland all played the piano in public; Hindemith played the viola and conducted; Messiaen played the organ weekly at La Trinité in Paris; and Stravinsky, Webern, Copland, Schoenberg, Bridge, Vaughan Williams and Tippett conducted (and not just their own works). Britten performed throughout most of his career until illness prevented him. While it is possible to find musicians and listeners who actively disliked or were merely indifferent to Britten's compositions, it is difficult to find those who had a bad word to say about his piano playing or conducting.

As with other aspects of his life, Britten's relationship with performing was complex. As a child he dominated the family piano, becoming upset when others had to have their turn, and his prowess was evidently a marvel at school. The competitor in him must have revelled in any opportunity to display his technical mastery. However, once he was an adult with a reputation to maintain, extreme tension could build up: Pears told Alan Blyth that Britten could, in his later years, '"freeze" before appearing on the platform'.[1] But performers clearly enjoyed working with him,[2] and recordings of Britten in rehearsal suggest that he enjoyed that behind-closed-doors process, at least.

It was as a conductor, inevitably, that he reached his largest live audience. He was not, though, entirely comfortable with the role. He directed the first performances of *Billy Budd* and *Prince of the Pagodas*, which both call on large forces, but in the first case took over from the indisposed Josef Krips,[3] and in the latter took the podium because the first-choice conductor, Ernest Ansermet, was not available – along with, presumably, the four other conductors who were, as he wrote to David Webster, 'on our list' (*LL4* 456). Imogen Holst, ever protective, was furious about the episode which she recalled to Donald Mitchell: 'He

---

[1] Alan Blyth, *Remembering Britten* (London: Hutchinson, 1981), 18.
[2] See, for example, the interviews with various performers, ibid.
[3] *LL3* 660.

was never meant to conduct *Prince of the Pagodas*. Covent Garden persuaded him against his will and said that they couldn't do it without him ... It wasn't only that his arm was bad but in those days he'd *no* experience of conducting a *huge* orchestra in a *very* long work in an orchestral pit for dance ...' (477). Britten's withdrawal from the last seven performances was on doctor's orders, having conducted only the first three.[4] From that point onwards he tended to avoid directing large ensembles in live performance; the first performance of his next opera, *Gloriana*, was conducted by John Pritchard, for instance, and for the first performance of *War Requiem* Britten took charge of the chamber orchestra, leaving the main orchestra and chorus to Meredith Davies. He was much more comfortable with the smaller forces and intimate atmosphere of the English Opera Group and the English Chamber Orchestra. As a pianist, he seems to have been happy to take the soloist's role in the first performances of his Piano Concerto, Op. 13 in 1938 (in front of the largest concert audience to be had in the UK, that of the Proms) and *Young Apollo* in 1939 (in Canada and New York). But he relinquished the spotlight after that, and in fact never wrote a major solo piano work for himself or anyone else.[5] He played duets with Richter during the Aldeburgh Festival, but was best known (and probably happiest) as an accompanist. He worked with Pears, chiefly, in performances of his own and others' songs, but also with Rostropovich – in his own Cello Sonata, and sonatas by Schubert (the 'Arpeggione'), Bridge and Debussy – and, briefly, Yehudi Menuhin, whom he accompanied on a tour of Germany just after World War II.

There was much touring, with the EOG and as accompanist. Increasingly, though, recording (principally with Decca) became the means by which he sustained his public. As Paul Kildea has documented, Britten's attitude towards the gramophone changed during the 1960s from the stance outlined in his Aspen Award speech, in which he bemoaned the possibility that 'at the turn of a switch' a work such as Bach's *St Matthew Passion* 'is at the mercy of any loud roomful of cocktail drinkers – to be listened to or switched off at will, without ceremony or occasion' (*BoM* 259–60). In fact the year before he delivered the speech he was writing to Ernst Roth:

---

[4] *LL4* 479.
[5] He wrote *Night Piece* (Notturno) in 1963 for the first Leeds Piano Competition, but this is hardly a major work.

12. *Britten conducts a rehearsal of his Cello Symphony with its dedicatee, Mstislav Rostropovich, in June 1964.*

> As you know, I value very highly the *authentic* recordings of my works, and wish to keep my contact with the Decca Company (who is most sympathetic to the idea) very close indeed ... It does not seem to be understood in the firm [Boosey & Hawkes] that these major recordings are to be encouraged in every way rather than to be regarded as a muisance [*sic*] ... (*SB* 226)

The success of the *War Requiem* recording no doubt helped to change his mind: it apparently sold two hundred thousand copies in the first five months.[6] The partnership with Decca led to the most complete recorded coverage of any composer born before World War I during their lifetime (certainly with the composer at the helm); and during the 1960s the record company made discs of Britten's new works as they were completed.[7] The recordings are still available, as downloads at least.[8] It is not invariably the case that a composer's own readings maintain benchmark status for subsequent generations, but it seems likely that Britten's will continue to do so: more recent recordings often have superior sound quality, and performances of the bigger works are sometimes more polished than Britten's own (standards of choral singing, in particular, have, generally speaking, risen since the

---

[6] *BB* 411.
[7] See *SB* 222–3.
[8] For the complete list see John Evans, Philip Reed and Paul Wilson (eds.), *A Britten Source Book* (Aldeburgh: The Britten Estate, 1987), 169–82.

mid-1970s), but Britten's are rarely outdone in terms of dramatic pacing (in all genres, not just opera), control of form, and the relation of detail to whole. Responses to Pears's voice, which features extensively in the legacy, are often sharply divided, and there are some things Pears can do better than others (naturally Britten tended to maximize those he was better at), but in terms of musical intelligence he leaves nothing to his rivals, contemporary or more recent.

Britten also recorded works by composers with whom he felt a particular affinity – Bach's Brandenburg Concertos and *St John Passion*, Mozart's piano concertos and symphonies, Schubert's songs (*Die Winterreise* and *Die schöne Müllerin* and various individual songs), and folksong arrangements by Grainger.[9] His collaborators in these were his favourites: Pears, of course, and Richter, Clifford Curzon, and the English Chamber Orchestra. Britten is not as readily associated with Schumann as with these other composers, but he recorded his *Dichterliebe* with Pears, as well as the *Scenes from Goethe's 'Faust'* (his last recording, during the sessions for which he was clearly in some difficulty from his heart problem) and his Cello Concerto. The soloist for the concerto was Rostropovich, whom Britten also accompanied in recordings of the various sonatas they performed in concert.

One would expect otherwise, but not all that much by Frank Bridge was set down, and no major works apart from the Cello Sonata. Britten recorded some of the songs of his official teacher, John Ireland, too, as well as one of Tippett's song-cycles, *Songs for Ariel* – though not the ones Tippett wrote for him and Pears, *Boyhood's End* and *The Heart's Assurance* (Pears did record it, but with Noel Mewton-Wood). Surprisingly, given Britten's attitude towards the composer, he agreed to play piano in a 1948 recording of Vaughan Williams's *On Wenlock Edge*. Pears, who sang the tenor part, must have managed to sway him on this occasion.

However, it must have been more than Pears's cajoling that led to the recording of *The Dream of Gerontius* in 1972. Britten had already dipped his toe in Elgarian waters in 1969 with a purely instrumental work, the Introduction and Allegro for strings. Presumably he was now seeing past the Imperialist persona lambasted in his diaries of the 1930s. Both Elgar's works benefit from Britten's unfussy, clear-sighted approach, with *Gerontius* notably shorn of the sentimentality and bombast that can creep in if inviting moments are indulged at the expense of the whole. As with Britten's composing, less, it seems, can be more. Particularly striking is the tempo for the final

---

[9] See Evans, Reed and Wilson (eds.), *A Britten Source Book*.

section of *Gerontius*, which is quicker than that of some of Elgar's best-known champions. Britten's basic tempo is in fact bang on Elgar's marking of quaver = 92; other recorded performances take it slower, sometimes markedly so. His performance reveals that the expansiveness of the melodic lines – the genuine sense of spaciousness that is surely of the essence here – comes across more certainly if played at a tempo that allows the listener to take in the shape of the lines properly.

Perhaps less likely to sustain an audience are Britten's performances of music now thought to be within the domain of early music specialists. Although there is the same placing of detail to whole to their mutual advantage in, for example, his 1972 recording of Purcell's *The Fairy Queen*, modern tastes are likely to find the sound of the English Chamber Orchestra a little heavy on its feet, and the range of nuances comparatively limited.

Special insight into Britten the performer is afforded by two commercially available recordings of rehearsals – for the Decca recording of *War Requiem* made in the wake of its first performance, and for a Canadian Broadcasting Corporation performance of the song-cycle *Nocturne*, Op. 60 with Pears and the CBC Vancouver Chamber Orchestra.[10]

The *War Requiem* rehearsals were recorded without Britten's knowledge and presented to him as a gift by the producer, John Culshaw. The excerpts are obviously selective, but are sufficient to convey a good impression of Britten's rehearsal technique, which is economical and rigorously to the point. He is strong on the observance of dynamic markings, and on pitch: when, for example, the first tenors are slightly out of tune in their second entry in the 'Pleni sunt coeli' section of the Sanctus, he remarks, 'There seems to be a slight difference of opinion amongst you about that C natural. Some of your C naturals were rather B-ish, if I may say so.' This comment is indicative of the dry humour that is used sparingly but effectively. As one might expect, much of his wit is directed at the Boys' choir: 'Can you start that section ['Te decet hymnus'] with more *enthusiasm*: it's a little bit early morningy. I know it *is* early morning but make it not sound early morning would you?'; and when, during the 'Hostias' section of the Offertorium, the boys struggle to keep to their note against the conflicting tenor and baritone soloists and chamber orchestra: 'It's supposed to be different. Don't make it sound nice – it's

---

[10] The *War Requiem* rehearsal is bundled with Britten's performance of the work, and is available as a download. The *Nocturne* performance is published by VAI Audio: VAI DVD 4277.

horrid, it's *modern* music.' When it transpires that the tuba player doesn't have his mute with him Britten is clearly irritated ('Well unfortunately we're not recording tomorrow we're recording *tonight*'), but the situation is diffused: 'Has anyone got a tuba mute? Chorus sit down while we consider the tuba mute. [Inaudible comment from the orchestra.] Well have we got any more handkerchiefs? ... You can have my coat to put in it.' He can be sharp, too: during the rehearsal of the first movement, Requiem aeternam, he shouts to the boys, who are clearly not fully attentive: 'Listen to what I'm saying chaps! *Listen!*' There is the intimation of a reservoir of explosive anger in the tone of this remark.

In a number of places he is concerned with establishing the right mood: in the Dies irae he wants 'hysteria please from everyone' and later complains, 'Chorus you sound much too healthy: there's no sound of terror about this. Make it sound creepy, make it sound *alarmed*,' while the entry of the chorus in the Offertorium should sound as if the singers are coming out of a dream. On one occasion he talks in explicitly structural terms, explaining the importance of the climax on 'Teste David cum Sibylla' just before the 'Lacrimosa', where he wants more tone: he states that this is almost the highpoint of the work because of the importance of the key of B flat minor, 'which is to go right the way through the "Lacrimosa"'.

The rehearsal of the *Nocturne* took place in a television studio in advance of a full performance, intercut with some comments from Pears on the poetry Britten set. It allows a study of his conducting technique, which, unsurprisingly, is unfussy, economical and clear – in that the beat is very easy to follow. The CBC Vancouver Chamber Orchestra plays well for him, even if the harpist, flautist and clarinettist have a little difficulty with precision in their *obbligati* sections. The rehearsal is business-like, the atmosphere concentrated rather than tense despite the presence of cameras. There is particular encouragement from Britten during the rehearsal of the cor anglais solo, played (very responsively) by the youngest member of the ensemble.

It is possible to be a major composer without performing at all (Elliott Carter and György Ligeti are two roughly contemporary examples), and the notion is surely debatable that composers who perform the music of others must have a privileged insight into it, simply because they push notes around on paper. Whether the two activities can genuinely be said to enhance each other in Britten's case is hard to prove (he rarely revised his scores on the basis of performing experience, unlike, say, Mahler). But his performance of a wide range of music – beyond concerns relatively close to his own compositional interests – is testimony to his belief in a composer's need to be thoroughly embedded in the musical culture in which he or she works.

FOUR

TEARING THE WASTE AWAY
(1960–1972)

If Britten's post-*Grimes* activity up to the late 1950s can be characterized as a period of expansion (with a particularly high rate of compositional production, and burgeoning administrative and performance duties associated with the Aldeburgh Festival and the EOG), one senses in the 1960s an increasing paring down – the distillation of the essentials in his life, personal and professional, in a relentless quest for maximum efficiency and the fulfilling of what he saw as his duty to music. There was an increasing focus on Aldeburgh as HQ, with other locations available when further retreat was needed (for example in Venice, or his house in Horham). Performances were undertaken with a small group of trusted collaborators, including the EOG, plus notable new ones – such as the Russian cellist Rostropovich, whom Britten first met in the Royal Festival Hall on 21 September 1960 (Rostropovich was giving the first performance of the Cello Concerto No. 1 by Shostakovich, whom Britten also met), and the German baritone Fischer-Dieskau. A coterie of support staff helped with the production line and kept the world at bay when it was not wanted. A particularly important member of the support staff was Rosamund Strode, who in 1964 took over from Imogen Holst as Britten's amanuensis. She observed in her interview with Carpenter that

> you simply had to protect [Britten] from certain people. There were the totally crazy people who sometimes turned up uninvited. And yes, there were people on his Christmas card list who nevertheless caused a groan when they were mentioned – though [Britten and Pears] … wouldn't have dreamt of cutting them out altogether. You might call it grit in the machinery. And a highly-tuned machine cannot stand grit.[1]

---

[1] BB 503.

In all this, contrary to the usual conception of the relationship between life and art, the former would appear to have reflected the latter. One particular aspect of Britten's aesthetics came to the fore in an interview in 1963 (one of the several he made in that decade) when the interviewer, Murray Schafer, noted that, in comparison with Berg, 'There is nothing of the heavy, lush effect with you.' Britten responded:

> Berg and Schoenberg share common ground in the respect of the complexity of their musical thought. The multiplication of parts in their music is often staggering. But I am at precisely the other end of music. Music for me is clarification; I try to clarify, to refine, to sensitize. Stravinsky once said that one must work perpetually at one's technique. But what is technique? Schoenberg's technique is often a tremendous elaboration. My technique is to tear all the waste away; to achieve perfect clarity of expression, that is my aim. (*BoM* 227)

There are positive and negative effects of 'tearing all the waste away'. The charge from some critics is that the music of this period is too pared down, while the reduction of the number of people Britten dealt with directly (and of the time that he was willing to give to meet with them) created a good deal of friction and resentment. The administrative streamlining was hardly surprising – indeed it was a necessity if he were to sustain his productivity at the pace he insisted on setting himself. And the creation of buffers between himself and the outside world was probably a way of trying to cope with his increasing public profile, which was fuelled by the huge success of one work in particular, *War Requiem*, as well as by his fiftieth-birthday celebrations. If his compositional output appears to dip (certainly in terms of total duration), this can in large measure be explained by illness – though Britten himself noted that he was finding it harder to compose, admitting to a BBC interviewer in 1963, 'It is becoming, as I get older, more and more difficult to satisfy my ear that I have found the right notes to express my ideas with ... I shall probably not write as much [in the future]. I can see that one is slowing down as one gets older.'[2]

'Make people think abit'

> What with illness, & the enforced rest of this summer, & the terrific job of M.S.N.D. [*A Midsummer Night's Dream*], there is no chance of doing that Sea Symphony for Leeds. I've got a busy winter (many postponed commitments from last year), & I'm due to do that big piece for Coventry by the Autumn or early Winter of 1961. I'm as sorry about this as you, but one day I'll do it, only it will take time, I fear. (*LL5* 225)

---

[2] *BB* 421.

I hate to disappoint you like this [postponing a 'Mahler' piece – presumably intended for the fiftieth anniversary of his death], especially as I feel such admiration for what you are doing at the BBC. (*BPL*)

These excerpts from letters to, respectively, Lord Harewood (19 May 1960) and William Glock, the controller of music at the BBC (30 July 1960), are early intimations to two key movers and shakers in the British musical world that Britten was gearing himself up for the work that arguably made the biggest impact of any, by any composer of any nationality, written during the 1960s: *War Requiem*, Op. 66 (1962), which intersperses settings of poems by Wilfred Owen within a setting of the Latin Mass for the Dead. No work of Britten's has polarized critical response to quite the same degree. It sums up Britten's art in many ways, and was surely viewed by the composer himself as one of his most important utterances.

The possibility that Britten might compose a work for the festival marking the consecration of the new cathedral in Coventry was first mooted in late 1958. Works by other composers were commissioned too (Tippett's second opera, *King Priam*, for example, plus Brian Easdale's *Missa coventrensis* and *The Beatitudes* by the Master of the Queen's Music, Arthur Bliss), but it was *War Requiem* that received most of the publicity. 'Hype' would not be an entirely inappropriate word to use. The centrality of Britten's work in the festival and the expectations surrounding it indicate his delayed emergence as an Establishment figure – 'delayed' because this might well have happened earlier if the first performance of *Gloriana* had been more successful. A number of articles about *War Requiem* were published pre-performance, and the consensus was that the audience was about to witness a masterpiece. Thus Alec Robertson in *The Musical Times*: 'Britten's finest work to date', 'this great work';[3] and William Mann ('Our Music Critic') in *The Times*, under the headline 'Britten's Masterpiece Denounces War': 'There is no doubt at all, even before next Wednesday's performance, that it is Britten's masterpiece.'[4] Britten himself referred to the work in such tones in a letter to Anthony Gishford of Boosey & Hawkes in April 1961: 'I am going into Purdah now, trying hard to get on with the new masterpiece for Coventry' (*BPL*). But he was clearly being sardonic.

Britten's use of the word 'masterpiece' does, though, indicate that he was aware of the expectations, and of his status. Certainly, as other, post-performance commentators observed, there is a sense of him gathering all his experience and technical resources in addressing a subject perhaps closest to his heart.[5] The performing forces are large: soprano, tenor and baritone soloists; large chorus; boys' choir accompanied by chamber organ;

---

[3] *The Musical Times*, vol. 103, no. 1431 (May 1962), 308–10.
[4] *The Times*, 25 May 1962.
[5] See, for example, Peter Evans, 'Britten's "War Requiem"', *Tempo*, 61/2 (1962), 20.

chamber orchestra; and large orchestra. They are disposed in three spatially separated domains: soprano, chorus and orchestra; boys and chamber organ; male soloists and chamber orchestra. The first two groups are confined to singing the words of the Mass, the last group the Owen poems.

Such is the work's canonic status, almost instantaneously gained, that it is often forgotten that it was conceived as an occasional piece. Indeed, *War Requiem* epitomizes Britten's attitude to the composer's role. Whatever life Britten envisaged for the work after its initial two performances in Coventry, it was clearly designed to have its maximum impact on a broadly based audience on the first hearing. The clear references to other composers' music – Verdi's own Requiem in the 'Lacrimosa', Bach's B minor Mass in the Sanctus (the swinging bass lines) – were likely not to be for connoisseurs' benefit, but intended to resonate with the ordinary, perhaps even the 'sometime', listener's experience. The notes were no less carefully selected than normal, but it tends to be the piece's broad effects that count the most (which, given the dreadful acoustics of the new building, is probably just as well). There are a number of spectacular accumulations of sound, such as in the Dies irae (the traditional cue for massed brass, here given a chilling military spin), in 'In paradisum' (a more luminous context, this, which employs possibly the densest texture in the work, with the greatest number of independent lines), and not least in the climactic G minor chord of 'Libera me' – which possibly trumps the B flat chord at the end of *Billy Budd* in sheer decibel level, if not sophistication of effect. However, the most intensely emotional moments are the simplest: the tenor soloist's 'Dona nobis pacem' at the end of the Agnus Dei (the only time he sings the Latin text[6]), for instance, and the baritone soloist's 'I am the enemy you killed my friend. I knew you in this dark' towards the end of 'Strange Meeting', just before 'In paradisum'. This is in effect the moment of reconciliation and is a simply decorated descending arpeggiation of a first-inversion G minor triad.

'Strange Meeting' was particularly charged at the first performance because Britten had invited Dietrich Fischer-Dieskau to sing the baritone part as an intended gathering of representatives of the three main European powers of World War II. Pears sang tenor, Fischer-Dieskau of course represented Germany, and the Russian Galina Vishnevskaya, Rostropovich's wife, was to have sung the soprano part, but the Soviet authorities denied her permission to do so and Heather Harper took her place at very short notice. On 16 February 1961 Britten had written to Fischer-Dieskau: 'Peter Pears has agreed to sing the tenor part, and with great temerity I am asking you whether you would sing the baritone' (*LL5* 313). The first performance took its toll on the baritone, Britten telling

---

[6] The insertion of the Latin text into the soloist's lines from Owen was Pears's idea: see Mervyn Cooke, *Benjamin Britten: War Requiem* (Cambridge: Cambridge University Press, 1996), 36.

William Plomer that 'Poor F-Dieskau was so upset at the end that Peter couldn't get him out of the choir-stalls!'[7]

But if 'Strange Meeting' and 'In paradisum' enact reconciliation, the ending of the work offers no easy comfort. The final passage of music is a chorale-like texture that has been heard twice before, to different texts – at the end of the Requiem aeternam and Dies irae movements. It is another passage in which less means more expressively, the simplicity prompted, as Peter Evans says, by the need for 'all elaboration of grief [to] be pruned away after Owen's exposure of its inadequacy'.[8] Punctuated by the tritone C–F sharp on tubular bells and cadencing initially on that interval, the chorale finally finds its way to a chord of F major. As in *Les illuminations* and *Peter Grimes*, the tritone is for Britten the epitome of conflict (its only rival is the semitonal dichotomy witnessed in, for example, *Billy Budd* and *The Turn of the Screw*). *War Requiem* is peppered with the interval from the very beginning, when the chorus intones the opening words, 'Requiem aeternam', on F sharp and C, at first alternately and then together. So the final relaxing on the most restful of musical sonorities ought to have a consoling effect. And yet the first time the passage is heard, at the end of Requiem aeternam, the F major triad sounds (contradictorily) surprising, inevitable – and unconvincing. At the moment the triad arrives one can accept it as the closure of this passage through some unorthodox logic, but it remains 'curiously disengaged', as Evans puts it,[9] from the structure as a whole. At the third appearance of the passage its outcome is no longer surprising, but the sense of 'disengagedness' is if anything reinforced.

War Requiem's closing pages, and indeed the work as a whole, might be regarded as a critique of Christianity, highlighting the inability of the religion's central rituals (and, by implication, its doctrines) to offer solace in the face of the suffering of the two world wars. The focus on Owen's poems renders the work decidedly humanitarian: as Brett has observed, the work employs Owen's poetry 'to transmit [Britten's] anger about the fate of young men sent to their deaths by an unfeeling patriarchal system as well as [critiquing] empty religious forms in collusion with that system'.[10] Britten's relationship with religious belief seems to have been equivocal. His diary entries around Easter Day 1936 show that he was no longer inclined to attend church – 'No one goes to Church early this morning. Subject is dropped like lead' (*JB* 345) – and Pears told Carpenter, 'I am not sure that he would really have called himself a Christian.'[11] Nevertheless Britten himself declared in a 1963 BBC interview (not long after the composition of *War Requiem*, naturally) 'I'm certainly a dedicated

---

[7] *BB* 410.
[8] Evans, 'Britten's "War Requiem"', 23.
[9] Peter Evans, *The Music of Benjamin Britten* (2nd edn, London: Dent, 1989), 464.
[10] *BBGO*.
[11] *BB* 113.

13. Britten standing in the nave of Coventry Cathedral before the premiere of War Requiem, *30 May 1962.*

Christian ... [though] at the moment I do not find myself worshipping as regularly as perhaps I will later.'

Of course, the main 'critique' in *War Requiem* is of war itself. Of Britten's previous anti-war pieces *Ballad of Heroes* is the most overt, but anti-war sentiment also plays a part in *Our Hunting Fathers* (with vermin allied to the Nazi party, and the hunting-dog names of 'German' and 'Jew'), the Violin Concerto (partly a reaction to the Spanish Civil War), *Sinfonia da Requiem* ('combining my ideas on war & a memorial for Mum & Pop', LL2 803), and *Canticle III: Still Falls the Rain*. In *War Requiem* the anti-war sentiment is obviously up-front; embodied in the work's very name, it is also in its motto, which quotes Owen: 'My subject is War, and the Pity of War. / The poetry is in the pity. / All a poet can do today is warn.' The sentiment is also the most sustained. During the 1950s Britten had begun to lend public support to various causes and was co-signatory to sixteen letters to *The Times* between 14 December 1950 and 23 January 1970. Some were on human rights issues (support for the abolition of hanging, for instance, and protesting against the banishment of the Greek composer Mikis Theodorakis), and five were on broadly pacifist themes: a protest against the use of napalm by the UN in Korea, and warnings about the threat of Soviet intervention in Czechoslovakia and the threat to Cornish moorland from its use by the Admiralty for military exercises. Others concerned the use of atomic weapons, and on 16 April 1952 he signed a letter proposing a 'pacific' representation at the Coronation as well as a military one. But for a composer the principal medium for any political message is going to be music, and this was the ideal time in Britten's career to put forward his concerns: not only was his profile such that *War Requiem* would attract a good deal of attention, but virtually two decades of operatic experience had equipped him for dealing with what was probably his biggest technical challenge to date.

Britten's letters to William Plomer and Peter Maxwell Davies soon after *War Requiem*'s first performance suggest a certain degree of satisfaction, hedged by Britten's habitual telling himself that he's not quite good enough:

> I was so pleased with your letter – & pleased that you heard 'War Requiem' and thought it did what it should. I am, at the moment, only too aware of where it falls short of the idea, which is so close to my heart. But it was an enormous task, & one is, after all, only human! (to WP, 5 June 1962, LL5 401)

> I was frankly nervous at attempting such a tremendous subject. Whether I have succeeded I can't tell – but anyhow it has had certainly a remarkable <u>extra</u>-musical success, which at any rate may make people think abit (to PMD, 18 November 1963, 523)

The critical reaction, and the reaction of audiences, was highly enthusiastic, Peter Shaffer going so far as to say that the 'profound and moving' climax of the work 'makes criticism impertinent'.[12] But among those disturbed by the level of praise was Stravinsky, who had requested a score of the work from Boosey & Hawkes on 15 February 1963:[13]

> The *War Requiem* is surely one of Britten's finest hours-and-a-half, and the reception accorded the music was a phenomenon as remarkable as the music itself. In fact the Battle-of-Britten sentiment was so thick and the tide of applause so loud that I, for one, was not always able to hear the music. Behold *The Times*, in actual, Churchillian quotes: 'Few recordings can ever have been awaited so eagerly and by so many people ... practically everyone who has heard it has instantly acknowledged it as a masterpiece ...' [...]
> Kleenex at the ready, then, one goes from the critics to the music, knowing that if one should dare to disagree with 'practically everyone', one will be made to feel as if one had failed to stand up for '*God Save the Queen*'. The victim of all this, however, is the composer, for of course nothing fails like success, or hurts more than the press's ready certification of a 'masterpiece'.[14]

This is not, if read literally, couched as criticism of the work as such. But one composer-critic who has not shirked from expressing his doubts is Robin Holloway, who in his 1977 Britten 'Memorial piece' explained that 'the public manner of *War Requiem* [seemed] a betrayal of the authentic voice of the *Serenade*, the *Nocturne*, the *Winter Words*.'[15] His views, reasserted in his *Spectator* column of 26 November 2008[16] (in which he complains of facile settings of the Owen poems and too much routine), are indicative of the doubts shared by a number of musicians and listeners in the early 1960s, even if they were not voiced so loudly as those of the acclaimers.

Some of the dissenters were no doubt spurred on by their reactions against what they saw as immoderate claims made for Britten's music in a book published in 1952, *Benjamin Britten: a Commentary on his Works from a Group of Specialists*.[17] This was edited by Donald Mitchell, who from 1963 had special responsibility for Britten's music at Boosey & Hawkes, and Hans Keller, an Austrian émigré who fled to London from the Nazis in 1938 and joined the BBC in 1959. Keller's advocacy of Britten's pre-eminence in the contemporary compositional world was particularly vociferous, equating Britten to Mozart. Britten thanked the editors at the beginning of 1953,

---

[12] *Time & Tide*, 7 June 1962, quoted in Cooke, *War Requiem*, 79.
[13] See Stephen Walsh, *Stravinsky. The Second Exile: France and America 1934–1971* (London: Pimlico, 2007), 657.
[14] Igor Stravinsky and Robert Craft, *Themes and Conclusions* (London: Faber & Faber, 1972), 26–7.
[15] Robin Holloway, *On Music: Essays and Diversions 1963–2003* (Brinkworth: Claridge Press, 2003), 209. See also his essay 'Benjamin Britten: the sentimental sublime', ibid.
[16] <http://www.spectator.co.uk/the-magazine/arts/3043381/let-down-by-britten.thtml>, accessed 4 September 2009.
[17] Donald Mitchell and Hans Keller (eds.), *Benjamin Britten: A Commentary on his Works from a Group of Specialists* (London: Rockcliffe, 1952).

noting that 'Of course you wouldn't believe me if I said I was equally pleased with every contribution', but he was delighted with 'the seriousness of it … & the admirable quality of a great deal of the contents, in which I would like to include both of your contributions' (*LL4* 119–20). To Imogen Holst, though, his reactions were slightly different:

> We talked about the book about him: – he said it made him feel like a small and harmless rabbit being cut up by a lot of grubby school-boys when he'd <u>much</u> rather be frisking about in the fields. I quoted one or two of Keller's inaccurate generalisations, and he said that it was distressing when people made arrogant statements … He said what a relief it was after wading through Keller on him … to go back to William [Plomer, whose poems he'd been reading when he couldn't get to sleep].[18]

We shouldn't perhaps make too much of Britten's duplicity regarding Keller's contribution: it is common enough human behaviour to say one thing when thinking another in order to smooth over relations (Britten did in fact form a good working relationship with Keller, to the extent that his last major work was dedicated to him), and this is particularly prevalent in a social class that puts a premium on avoiding face-to-face unpleasantness at virtually all costs. Apart from one or two exceptional instances, Britten appears to have been a strong subscriber to this approach. But this doesn't mean that he didn't publicly hit out at critics en masse: in the same year that Mitchell and Keller's book was published Britten contributed an article to *Opera* in which he gave full rein to his views as to what sort of work critics should do, and what type of person they should be. He ends with a plea that the critic should possess

> *real* knowledge, not this half-learning which prevents a person reacting in the simple way, and yet doesn't give him technical assistance to understanding. Again, please let us have humility. We are not writing or performing for the critic, let him remember … it is the public we are there for; they are open minded and, if we can deliver the goods and have the goods to deliver, friendly and sympathetic as well.[19]

This may be well reasoned, but testimony from those who worked with Britten supports the view that he had a tendency to overreact to criticism. Because of this, and his tendency also to shun discussion of the technical specifics of his music, he acquired a reputation for viewing such matters with some disdain. It is, however, a reputation that needs a little finessing. In November 1962 Mitchell sent Britten the latest issue of Boosey & Hawkes's in-house journal, *Tempo*, of which he was then the editor. Conceived as an eightieth-birthday tribute for Stravinsky, the issue mostly

---

[18] *LL4* 121.
[19] *BoM* 118.

featured articles on the Russian, but Mitchell tentatively introduced to Britten another item: 'I hope you will get something out of the article on the "War Requiem" by Peter Evans. I think he is a very talented writer about your music and we have asked him at Faber's to undertake a full length study. I hope the prospect won't horrify you. Perhaps we might have a talk about this when we next meet' (*BPL*). Despite its relatively modest length, Evans's article was the most searching and insightful writing on Britten's music to that date, and the composer's reply to Mitchell – 'I think P. Evans rather good!' (*LL5* 435) – suggests that it was the quality of the critical undertaking, as he perceived it, that was his issue with criticism and critics.[20]

As regards Holloway's view of *War Requiem*, it is by no means certain that Britten would have disagreed with many of his misgivings, given the contents of his letters to Plomer and to Maxwell Davies, and also the careful statement in a letter to his sister Beth that he thought the 'idea' of the *War Requiem* had 'come off I think'[21] (the emphasis on 'idea' is also seen in the letter to Maxwell Davies and was apparently reiterated to others). This suggests he was not entirely satisfied. And if Stravinsky's remark about nothing failing like success referred to scepticism that anything popular couldn't be truly profound (not Holloway's stance, it is however prevalent among apologists for modernism), there is evidence that Britten, too, was distrustful of the work's success. For, as several commentators have noted, subsequent works tended to explore more private spheres. This is even the case in much of his next significant work, the Symphony for Cello and Orchestra, Op. 68 (1963), which was ostensibly in the most public of genres.

The change of register could, though, be said to have been waiting in the wings before *War Requiem* was completed, since Britten only met the festival deadline by postponing work on the piece that effected the greatest degree of change in his compositional outlook in his career: the 'Parable for Church Performance', *Curlew River*, Op. 71 (1964). It involved substantial paring down, even by Britten's standards, and required a performing and listening environment in which the smallest events could derive momentous expressive impact.

'Very few movements'

Curlew River was the direct outcome of Britten's 1955–6 tour to the Far East in that it is what might be called a re-imagining of the Japanese Nō play *Sumidagawa*. As well as having seen the play twice in Tokyo, he had a

---

[20] Two other references to Evans in Britten's letters of 1964 support the composer's view of his work, with Britten saying 'I have such a high regard for him', again to Mitchell (*LL5* 617), and, to Jonathan Harvey, congratulating him on his appointment to the Southampton department: 'I hear the nicest things about Peter Evans' (*BPL*).
[21] *BB* 412.

recording made. In a broadcast on Japanese radio recorded at the beginning of December 1957, Britten stated that hearing the Nō play was 'among the greatest theatrical experiences of my life': 'The deep solemnity and *selflessness* of the acting, the perfect shaping of the drama (like a Greek tragedy) coupled with the strength and universality of the stories are something every Western artist can learn from.' He also mentioned the impact of Imperial Court Music (Gagaku), saying that he and Pears were 'impressed immediately by the great beauty of the sound, especially of that wonderful instrument the *shō*, by the stately melodies, and the subtlety of the rhythms'.[22]

It was William Plomer, who lived in Japan in his twenties, who had recommended that Britten should see some Nō plays, and it was to him that the composer turned for a libretto when, in mid-1957, he formed the intention to write a work based on *Sumidagawa*.[23] At first the scenario was to be close to the Japanese original, but on 15 April 1959 Britten sent Plomer a letter suggesting a new direction: 'the idea of making it a <u>Christian</u> work' and setting it in medieval England. One reason for the change was that he had been '<u>very</u> worried lest the work should seem a <u>pastiche</u> of a Noh play, which however well done, would seem false & thin' (*LL5* 130) – this despite his feeling in November 1958 that 'we should stick as far as possible to the original style & look of it' (87). What they kept was the outline of the story, of a mother seeking her lost son (though her 'release' on finding his grave and communing with his spirit was an alteration from the original, in which she remained mad); the ritualization, including the severe acting style (involving the use of masks) in which small movements can derive great significance; the small chamber ensemble, with a central role for flute and drums echoing the bamboo flute and drums of the original; the all-male cast; and the robing ceremony (again, highly ritualized). Transplanted from Gagaku are the sonorities of the *shō* (which are characterized by clusters – adjacent notes of the scale played together to form harmonies), transliterated for chamber organ, and certain technical features. Not only the acting style but also the form of the work is highly ritualized. A number of frames are employed, pivoting around the central storytelling as follows: procession – prologue – robing – the story – disrobing – moral/epilogue – recession.

Curlew River had a long gestation period, first postponed so that Britten could work on *A Midsummer Night's Dream*, then further delayed because (as he explained to Plomer on 1 January 1961[24]) he needed firstly to slow down a bit for health reasons, and also compose *War Requiem*. He finally got

---

[22] *BoM* 156–7.
[23] See Mervyn Cooke's extended account of the fascinating evolution of the libretto in Mervyn Cooke, *Britten and the Far East* (Woodbridge: Boydell Press and The Britten-Pears Library, 1997), 137–53.
[24] *BPL*.

around to writing the notes during January to March 1964, in Venice. While the relatively brief period of actual composition suggests he worked fluently, there were still significant problems to be solved, as he indicated to Donald Mitchell at the beginning of February: 'Apart from finding the right notes (& because there are so few of them, it seems harder than ever), one of the problems is how to write it down: there being no conductor, & the tempo is a kind of "controlled floating"' (*LL5* 552).

This sums up the essence of the work very well. Britten obviously responded so positively to Nō because of his 'less is more' aesthetic. But while his focus on 'tearing all the waste away' was first made public in 1963, when *Curlew River* was gestating under the surface, it had been fundamental to his practice since the word go. A statement in a letter to Erwin Stein a few months after the first performance of *Gloriana* in 1953 confirms that it was consciously sought:

> what I'm pleased with, and what has got people down, is the simplicity and directness, the fewness of the notes. This has been confused with thinness of invention. Time will show if they are right about this, but from a point of view of attitude or technique I'm sure I'm right, for this work at any rate. There is also room in the world for [Berg's] Lulu. (*LL4* 200)

But if *Curlew River* reinforced one tendency that was well established, the 'controlled floating' was certainly new. It stems from a rethinking of the role of harmony that intersects in some ways with the most revolutionary notion of Schoenberg's thinking – 'the unity of musical space'. This was the reconceptualization of the relationship between melody and harmony so that melody can become harmony, and harmony melody. Harmony becoming melody might not seem particularly revolutionary, since many melodies are based on the arpeggiation of chords; but these are usually elaborated by scale-steps (notes in between the thirds of the triads) or by what theorists call 'non-harmony notes'. What Schoenberg proposed was that anything that could be used as melody could be used as harmony. This notion is central to twelve-tone serial technique, with its deployment of segments of the series as melody or 'verticalized' as harmony. The most obvious manifestation of 'the unity of musical space' in *Curlew River* is the use of heterophony, which along with the *shō* is the work's chief indebtedness to Gagaku (though it is also present in gamelan music). Heterophony may be described as the simultaneous presentation of two or more versions of the same melody. One version might be more elaborate than the others, and they might all be slightly differently rhythmicized. The effect is similar to a church congregation (a body that is invariably not particularly well co-ordinated) singing 'in unison' in a resonant church.

A vital concomitant of jettisoning traditional distinctions between the horizontal and the vertical is the abandonment of the traditional distinction between consonance and dissonance, and therefore between tension and release – and, as the final consequence, a traditional sense of progression. 'Moving forward', when it occurs, is more a case of the dynamic of melodic movement and/or textural expansion and accumulation. As far as the listening experience is concerned this promotes focus on 'the moment', rather than projecting into a possible future on the basis of the known past – something that is of the essence in listening to, say, Beethoven. In this sense *Curlew River* represents Britten's closest approach to the avant-garde (Stockhausen was much involved during this period in what he described as 'Moment Form', for instance).

In Britten's interviews and speeches from the early 1960s he reinforces his stance that what his more 'progressive' colleagues were offering lacked much with which listeners could engage (certainly in a sustained way) and often created needless problems for performers:

> Often, looking at so-called 'avant garde' scores, it seems as if the notation has acquired some mystic value of its own. As a performer I resent wasting my time unravelling a notation which should be helping rather than hindering me, & which has no earthly effect aurally, except to produce inaccuracy & tensions. These, if wanted, should be calculated musically, not by accident. (*BoM* 238)

> [Re serialism:] It has simply never attracted me as a method, although I respect many composers who have worked in it, and love some of their works. It is beyond me to say why, except that I cannot feel that tonality is outworn, and find many serial 'rules' arbitrary. 'Socially' I am seriously disturbed by its limitations. I can see it taking no part in the music-lover's music-making. Its methods make writing *gratefully* for voices or instruments an impossibility, which inhibits amateurs and children. (228–9)

> … the *techniques* have become so frightfully interesting to people, and not the actual thing they say. Every time one steps out of an aeroplane one is asked by the journalists, 'what do you think of this style or that style of serial technique or electronics?', and one's reaction is always the same: It's not the style that interests me, it's what the chaps say writing in the style. The language is important as long as it conveys what the man has to say to me. But the language itself is a means to an end and not the end itself. (271)

Fed up with publicity

Britten's main public statement on his personal aesthetics was a speech he gave on 31 July 1964 when receiving the first Aspen Award from the Aspen Institute for Humanistic Studies in Colorado, the citation for the award being: 'To Benjamin Britten, who, as a brilliant composer, performer, and interpreter through music of human feelings, moods, and thoughts, has truly inspired man to understand, clarify and appreciate more fully his

14. A break from composing: Britten looks out of the window of his study in the Red House, June 1964.

own nature, purpose and destiny.'[25] The early 1960s – not insignificantly after Vaughan Williams's death in 1958, and before Tippett's profile rose to its height – was the period in which Britten became firmly established as the figurehead of British composition. Various honours, including the Order of Merit (1965), came his way,[26] and his fiftieth birthday in 1963 was widely celebrated (marred though the day itself was by the assassination of President Kennedy). He seems, though, if various statements to friends and colleagues are taken at face value, to have been unhappy about being in the spotlight. Just before his actual birthday he complained to William Plomer, 'I feel that my age at the moment is centenarian, rather than demi-c., & that these concerts are memorial rather than celebratory, & these nice things being written are really obituaries. I know what it's like to be dead, now' (*LL5* 526).

His reaction was to reinforce old barriers, and retreat into worlds he had carefully constructed around himself such as the Aldeburgh Festival, the EOG and the Red House itself. An indication of this can be seen in a letter

---

[25] *BoM* 255, note 2. See also extracts from Britten's speech in this book's Introduction, in which I identify Britten's views on the composer's role in society as being the anchoring theme of his career.

[26] A full list of Britten's honours and prizes can be found in John Bridcut, *The Faber Pocket Guide to Britten* (London: Faber & Faber, 2010), 131–4.

to Pears in July 1963: 'in future you must <u>never</u> do a damn thing that you don't want to – see? Life's too short for all this TV & bad conductor business [Pears was appearing in concerts and television recordings in Germany at the time]. Let's build up Aldeburgh into a real centre, & do all the things there we want to' (*LL5* 481–2). He built new barriers, too, with his alternative havens in Venice and, from 1970, in Horham, Suffolk, where his house was a retreat from the retreat, so to speak, for when he needed to distance himself from the demands associated with the Red House and the noise of the USAF jets that flew in and out of RAF Bentwaters.[27] A different kind of haven was established when, after a build-up of frustration with their handling of his catalogue and the direction of the company in general, Britten left Boosey & Hawkes in 1964 for a new venture, Faber Music, set up specifically – at least, initially – to publish his music, beginning with *Curlew River*.[28] Perhaps it was the establishment of the new publisher that stimulated Britten's expressions of hope for the future of English music, which he expressed in a letter to Peter Maxwell Davies on 18 November 1963 ('I think things are going to start happening musically in this country soon – & that isn't just a vague hope' (523)) and in an interview in *The Times* in late 1964:

> On the future of British music Mr. Britten was optimistic and encouraging – 'the best generation we've had for hundreds of years'. He named a few of the younger composers whose talent impresses him – Malcolm Williamson, Alexander Goehr, Nicholas Maw, Peter Maxwell Davies ('immensely gifted'), Richard Rodney Bennett ('I'm looking forward to his new opera, which he has very kindly dedicated to me'). 'What is so good is that they are all obeying their own musical impulses, not just blindly following what their foreign contemporaries are doing.'[29]

In harness?

In the same interview Britten was asked whether in *Curlew River* the 'use of cannon[30] and echo effects, and "non-alignment"' were to be understood as being 'suggestive of future paths' or 'specific for the subject and its treatment'? He responded with: 'I can't say; the technique always stems from the actual work you're writing. *Curlew River* had to take the special shape it did; and writing it has certainly broadened my technique. No, I'm too naive a person to say what its style may or may nor portend.'[31] The last sentence could be thought not a little disingenuous since, a matter of

---

[27] Britten wrote to the US Ambassador in June 1959 requesting that 'as few aeroplanes as possible fly over the district' during Festival performances (*LL5* 149).

[28] See *LL5* 574–6.

[29] *The Times*, 14 Dec. 1964.

[30] No doubt amusing to the pacifist composer when (or if) he read it, this should obviously be 'canon'.

[31] *The Times*, 14 Dec. 1964.

weeks after the first performance, he was writing to Plomer: 'Got a good idea for another opera in the same style [*The Burning Fiery Furnace*, Op. 77 (1966)] – so be prepared!'[32] And he must also have had some notion of how the new techniques might be incorporated or developed in the future. But, as always, his confidence easily waned, and he had at least one episode of beating himself up, writing to Pears on 17 November 1964, the month before the *Times* interview: 'I've been madly low & depressed – you being away mostly I expect, but worried about my work which seems so bad always ... I <u>must</u> get a better composer some how – but how – – – but how – –?' (*LL5* 614). Again, it is difficult to know whether this is a genuine crisis or Britten's means of checking that he's working hard enough, co-opting others into the process. But it might be why he and Pears decided to take a sabbatical in 1965. It was not, though, a sabbatical from composition – or at least, that is what he told *The Times* in December 1964:

> Oh no, most certainly not. It's that Peter Pears and I aren't doing concerts in the usual way, except regular engagements, of course, like the Aldeburgh and Long Melford festivals, and Peter's annual Matthew Passions. We're going to have six weeks in India, at the beginning of the year, and a trip to Russia in August (we're driving down to the Black Sea with Rostropovich and his wife); these will be entirely holiday.[33]

As it turned out, neither the Indian nor the Russian trip was 'entirely holiday': he wrote the (admittedly slight) *Gemini Variations*, Op. 73 in India for the 13-year-old twins Zoltán and Gábor Jeney, and in Russia a song-cycle for high voice and piano to texts by Pushkin, *The Poet's Echo*, Op. 76, for Vishnevskaya and Rostropovich (who was also a capable pianist).

In between these works he wrote *Songs and Proverbs of William Blake*, Op. 74, composed in April 1965 to a sequence of texts selected by Pears, and a rather faceless anthem to commemorate the twentieth anniversary of the UN, *Voices for Today*. *Songs and Proverbs* was written for and dedicated to Fischer-Dieskau, and is evidence that Britten did indeed have some clear ideas about how the '*Curlew River* experience' could be incorporated into his general approach to composition. This is most obvious in the settings of the Proverbs of Hell and aphorisms from the Auguries of Innocence that provide what Peter Evans calls the 'ritornelli' between the settings of the Songs of Experience: baritone and piano proceed independently of each other in the 'controlled floating' manner of *Curlew River*. The piano's material in all the ritornelli is based on the same twelve-tone series, which is divided into three four-note segments and used as a kind of 'pitch fund'; not all the segments are always used, and the order of the notes is often changed. The baritone draws on more

---

[32] BB 440.
[33] *The Times*, 14 Dec. 1964.

and more of the fund, until it uses all of it in the final aphorism, 'To See a World in a Grain of Sand' – the sentiment of which may be seen as another assertion of Britten's compositional ideal. This is one way in which Britten creates a sense of culmination across the work. Another comes from the material of the final song tangibly arising out of the preceding aphorism.

The final song is also a culmination – or perhaps a distillation (or perhaps both, simultaneously) – in the sense that Blake's text sums up the poetic issues of the cycle as a whole. In many ways *Songs and Proverbs* is Britten's darkest cycle, highlighting social ills and hypocrisies which were as much part of 1960s society (and ours today) as Blake's. As is usually the case with Britten, much of the imagery has an immediate impact: the search for a definitive point of repose in the first song, 'London', for instance ('I wander thro' each charter'd street'), or the repeated patterns, incessant tread and constant returns symbolizing Eternity in the last song, 'Every Night and Every Morn'. The symbolism of 'London' draws on a pun: the cadences are rootless in the musical sense that the main cadence points are first-inversion triads. The point is emphasized to ironic effect because the triads emerge from blurred scales in the piano as instances of sonorous clarity.

As in *War Requiem*, Britten employs the full range of available textural densities, achieving just about as much textural fullness as is possible in 'A Poison Tree' (it is, after all, about accumulating anger), while the final proverb employs the most minimal material and action. In his song-cycle *The Poet's Echo*, however, sparseness is as palpable a force as in *Curlew River*. Given that three songs, including the first and the last, are about absence – of a reply to the poet – the famished mien would seem to be an essential part of the work's 'message'. The notion of 'echo' might be thought to provide the perfect opportunity for the further development of heterophony. In fact Britten only comes close to this in the first song, actually entitled 'Echo', in which he employs a cross-fertilization of heterophony and canon (close canon with the rhythm frequently altered in subsequent voices).

The third of the post-*Curlew River* song-cycles, *Who are these Children?*, Op. 84 (1969), settings of William Soutar's poems in English and Scots dialect, is also epigrammatic, to the extent of including two riddles. It is perhaps the settings of the English poems ('Nightmare', 'Slaughter' and, especially, 'The Children') that are the most disturbing in their depiction of violence and its consequences, but the final, two-page setting of 'The Auld Aik' must count as one of Britten's most desperate utterances. The 'certainty' of the old world of common-practice tonality (The Old Oak) is deconstructed – in fact, dismantled – before our ears as the most familiar and comfortable chords of the work are isolated from each other by being placed in disconnected registers.

Particularly harsh in its sound-world is *Children's Crusade*, Op. 82 (1969), for children's voices, two pianos, percussion and electronic organ (the role of which is mostly to support the voices in writing that pushes the young singers to the limits). Britten himself referred to the work as 'a very grisly piece', and the subject-matter is indeed grim – a group of children try to flee the 'wilderness of night' that was Poland at the beginning of World War II, searching for peace but becoming lost without trace. The setting of the Bertolt Brecht text offers little in the way of lyrical possibilities. It does, though, offer a glimpse of hope – a suggestion of redemption through suffering in what Peter Evans describes as Britten's 'warmest Lydian-cum-Mixolydian vein'[34] – before the closing disintegration of this rather overlooked piece reminds us starkly of the reality of the continuing threat to the vulnerable.

Some have seen the sparseness of these works as deeply problematic, however – less as less, rather than more. Making a general comment on Britten's music, T. W. Adorno laid into the 'triumphant meagerness of Benjamin Britten', which demonstrated a 'taste for tastelessness, a simplicity resulting from ignorance, an immaturity which masks as enlightenment, and a dearth of technical means'.[35] And Robin Holloway sees in the post-*War Requiem* works a kind of musical anorexia: 'there is a point where the paradox of less-because-more becomes strained',[36] while the composer Robert Saxton (who corresponded with Britten for a while about his own compositions) has said that he felt at the time that Britten's music of the 1960s was 'icy and closed in'.[37]

Generally speaking, the music of the period sees subject and technique appropriately matched, and the best music is equivalent in richness to that of earlier periods. However, Holloway has a point when he refers to the 'steeply diminishing returns of the two church parables'.[38] Both contain some fine invention and deft characterization (particularly when it involves the 'bad guys' – the 'Merodak'-worship music in *The Burning Fiery Furnace*, and the Devil's music in *The Prodigal Son*, for example), but *The Prodigal Son*, in particular, has the air about it of a retread. In fact Britten, too, had his doubts. The business of composition started well enough (much of it was done in his beloved Venice) but was later hampered by illness, as he explained to Plomer on 29 April 1968:

> By breaking all doctors' orders, & really thrashing my poor old self, I have finished Prodigal Son – score & all. I <u>hope</u> it's all right, worthy of the wonderful subject & you, but under the circumstances I've done all I can & I hope you & God will forgive any inadequacies (of which I fear there are many). It is sickening that it had to be the most

[34] Evans, *The Music of Benjamin Britten*, 291.
[35] Theodor W. Adorno, *Philosophy of Modern Music*, trans. Anne G. Mitchell and Wesley V. Bloomster (London: Sheed & Ward, 1973), 7.
[36] Holloway, *On Music: Essays and Diversions*, 228.
[37] BB 535.
[38] Holloway, *On Music: Essays and Diversions*, 217.

difficult & important bit of the whole work which remained to be done – still, we shall see what we shall see … (*LL6* 216)

Britten was plagued by illness during the 1960s to an even greater extent than in the preceding decade, culminating in an operation for diverticulitis in February 1966 while he was in the middle of writing the full score of *The Burning Fiery Furnace*. Pears's support during this time was clearly of great significance, as this letter to him of 3 April 1966 shows:

It may not seem like it to you, but what you think or feel is really the most important thing in my life. It is an unbelievable thing to be spending my life with you: I can't think what the Gods were doing to allow it to happen! You have been so wonderful to me, given me so much of your life, such wonderful experiences, knowledge & wisdom which I never could have approached without you. And above all – your love, which I never have felt so strongly as in the lowest moments, physically & spiritually, of that old op. (*LL6* 23)

Britten's poor health was still a problem over a year later. Combined with the exhaustion of conducting a recording for Decca of *Billy Budd*, it necessitated his declining an invitation from Glock to conduct the BBC Symphony Orchestra (17 December 1967): 'I have run up against a bit of a physical crisis at the moment, & my doctor is making me take it very seriously. I must do less next year, otherwise I shall start letting people down at a dangerously late date' (*BPL*). The illness that flared up during the composition of *The Prodigal Son* was eventually diagnosed as sub-acute

15. Grand opening, 2 June 1967: Britten escorts the Queen to the inaugural concert at Snape Maltings. With them, left to right, are Peter Pears, Imogen Holst and Prince Philip.

endocarditis – an indication of the heart condition that eventually led to his death.

No doubt his illness was exacerbated by his workload, the non-compositional part of which was as heavy as ever: in addition to his visits to the Soviet Union there were tours to the US and to Central and South America (September 1967), a recital tour to New York (October 1969), an EOG tour to Australia followed by recitals in New Zealand (spring 1970), plus recordings for Decca of new works[39] (and works of other composers), and for BBC TV recordings of *Peter Grimes*, *Billy Budd* and *Owen Wingrave*. The biggest project of any kind during this period, though, was the renovation of The Maltings at Snape, a few miles from Aldeburgh, to provide a new concert hall for the Festival. Much of this took place without Britten's direct input – it was largely overseen by the Festival's General Manager, Stephen Reiss – but he was considerably involved in the planning process and fund-raising. The successful completion of the project in time for the 1967 Festival must have been energizing. The burning down of the hall during the 1969 Festival naturally had a rather different effect. It was just after this tragic event that Britten wrote to Yehudi Menuhin, rather despairingly, 'I am up to my eyes in work … a position made doubly difficult by the complications following the Maltings disaster.'[40] And in a BBC2 interview with John Tusa broadcast on 1 January 1970, in which he spoke candidly about the burden of worry, he admitted that he was 'Very depressed quite frankly' about starting the fund-raising process all over again.[41] Asked about the amount of time demanded by administration and fund-raising, he replied: 'Well one's life without administration is a very, very full one. And up 'til now one's been able to do it – to combine the two activities fairly easily. There have been clashes, I must admit, but now, with this *big* planning operation coming, the battle is already lost, I would say.' To the question of whether the squeeze affected the quality of what he composed, he responded:

> I don't think actually it does; of course it affects the *quantity* of what I write, and that is the worrying thing, because actually the way I work is basically to plan ahead and then find the time to write it down; so if the time doesn't come to write it down I don't think it makes the quality of the work any worse, but of course sometimes hurry can compel you to leave things that you're perhaps not very happy about. (*BoM* 340–41)

The '*big* planning operation' was in fact for an extension of the Maltings into a complex to include a music school, as well as an opera house and (as the report from the architects, Arup Associates, stated) 'facilities for

---

[39] See *SB* 222–3, which lists the dates of recording.
[40] *BB* 494.
[41] *BoM* 340.

other performing arts, such as dance and drama'. Clearly Britten liked a challenge, and was piling up even more work for himself (though not all the plans were realized) – but it is not difficult to understand his wish to seize opportunities for the improvement of his own and others' musical environment, and the disaster of the fire offered just such an opportunity.

Britten's life by the end of the 1960s could readily be characterized as being determined by various mechanisms and constraints set up largely by himself: the Festival needed consideration year in, year out; he was intent on keeping up his appearances with Pears on the concert platform and recording his music for Decca; and his various public statements about his artistic credo had to be lived up to. There was a weight of public expectation. His acute awareness of this might explain a remarkable statement he made to the Australian artist Sydney Nolan during the EOG's tour to the latter's native country. The statement came in a conversation, Nolan says, that revealed

> a side of him that I had never actually seen. And it lasted for about an hour and a half, and we had about three brandies. I was kind of overwhelmed by this revelation of his identity, of his character. And then we were due to land at Cairns for the Barrier Reef in about twenty minutes and he suddenly said, 'Well, that's the end of that. When I get back to England I won't be like that any more. My destiny is to be in harness and to die in harness'.[42]

Being 'in harness' could simply mean having a compulsion to work in the way he did, fulfilling his (by now extensive) duties as he saw them, or it could mean being constricted by certain personality traits that inevitably fed into his work. This chimes with Brett's statement that 'In returning to social protest in connection with boyhood at the end of the 1960s, he was all but announcing that his obsessions were what made him function.'[43] If this is the case, his agreement to collaborate with Nolan in the early 1970s on a television project on the subject of The Ancient Mariner (the figure-in-harness *nonpareil*) seems a remarkable statement of assent to these obsessions – though in the event it wasn't made because of Britten's failing health.[44] Or being 'in harness' could refer to his homosexuality. This was no longer illegal in 1970, of course, but the law change came too late for Britten to depart from the habits of a lifetime. More darkly, he might have been referring to the need to control his desire for pubescent boys – though it might be questioned whether Britten was on sufficiently close terms with Nolan even to hint at this to him.

When he made his 'in harness' statement to Nolan, Britten was about to start work on the second of his operas based on a Henry James story,

---

[42] BB 497.
[43] BBGO.
[44] LL5 166, 464.

Owen Wingrave, Op. 85 (1970), his final pacifist statement. Perhaps he was identifying with the protagonist, who escapes the suffocating weight of family expectation by making a stand against accusations of cowardice by locking himself overnight in a haunted room, which leads to his death by an unseen ghostly hand. Possibly there was some intimation of his own death in his statement to Nolan, too: while he had apparently recovered fully from the 1968 endocarditis, in 1960 his doctor had 'found evidence of aortic valve disease', and what Britten called his 'wonky heart' restricted his tennis playing. In August 1972 he was diagnosed with aortic incompetence, the consequences of which were to have a profound effect.

16. *Britten conducting at the Promenade concerts in the mid-1960s.*

Britten and Tippett

> For better or worse, we two are the most interesting English music has at the moment.[1]

Of all the composers Britten knew, Tippett is the one with whom he is most often bracketed and compared.[2] This is hardly surprising, given their closeness in age and the other points of connection between them – their shared scepticism of the previous generation of English composers, their interest in Purcell, the left-wing flavour of their politics, their pacifism (Britten and Pears famously visited Wormwood Scrubs to give a recital when Tippett, who had violated the terms of his registration as a conscientious objector, was an inmate there[3]), their adoption of aspects of European modernism, and their homosexuality (though this was never explicitly acknowledged by Britten during his lifetime, and not generally known of Tippett until the 1980s). It is clear that they recognized each other as fellow travellers, but also that they were aware of their differences and, in Tippett's case, at least, seem to have sought to emphasize them.

There is surprisingly little to be gleaned about Britten's view of Tippett. Just after meeting him in 1943 he wrote to Elizabeth Mayer describing him as a 'great new friend Peter & I have made, an <u>excellent</u> composer, & most delightful & intelligent man' (LL2 1151), but apart from his tribute to Tippett on the occasion of his sixtieth birthday[4] there is little indication from Britten's own mouth of what he thought of the man and his music. Presumably there were views passed in private that were not quite so complimentary as those related to Elizabeth Mayer. Imogen Holst noted in a diary entry from 11 October 1952 that Britten

> had doubts about Michael's 'Heart's assurance' songs [*The Heart's Assurance* (1950–51)]: – it was the first time he'd heard them from the outside [previously he'd been at the piano, accompanying Pears], and they didn't always make sense. He said he always knew what Michael was feeling in his music, and it moved him, but he didn't think Michael always managed to convey what he was thinking. We

---

[1] Letter from Tippett to Britten, 29 January 1955, in Thomas Schuttenhelm (ed.), *Selected Letters of Michael Tippett* (London: Faber & Faber, 2005), 205.
[2] See, for example, Arnold Whittall, *The Music of Britten and Tippett: Studies in Themes and Techniques* (2nd edn, Cambridge: Cambridge University Press, 1990).
[3] See *BB* 194.
[4] See *BoM* 274.

discussed the difficult ending of the last song and he said it was impossible vocally, and that he was sure the trouble was that the <u>notes</u> were wrong: – it was a weak cadence.[5]

Perhaps, constantly feeling wounded himself by public criticism of his music, Britten decided to keep most of his views on the work of others to his trusted circle.

There is rather more from Tippett about Britten – not surprisingly, since he outlived him into an age in which the private was beginning to become more solicited, or simply 'outed', for public consumption, and because he was interviewed by Carpenter for his Britten biography. The difference in the two composers' personalities is starkly revealed in Tippett's providing the kind of information to Carpenter that it is difficult to imagine Britten thinking entirely proper: 'Once [during World War II], Peter had to go off to London to sing and Ben remained behind. He thought it would be nice if we slept together, which we did, though I drew back from sexual relations; Peter was nevertheless quite disturbed at our intimacy on that occasion.'[6] He had criticisms, too, of a perceived change of attitude from Britten after the success of *Peter Grimes* and of the atmosphere at Aldeburgh:

> That great opera marked the turning-point in his career, and from then on he was less accessible, less ready to accept jokes or irreverence in relation to himself, his work or Peter; but he never betrayed his sense of vocation or his artistic integrity. Many close friends fell foul of Ben and Peter at Aldeburgh, which was sad. I realised what was going on and stayed apart from it all: if I went, subsequently, to the Aldeburgh Festival, I would send him a postcard saying I'd be there, but since no doubt he was busy, I wouldn't expect to see him. After his death, I was once invited to stay with Peter at the Red House, but found the reverent, mausoleum atmosphere oppressive.[7]

His obituary tribute to Britten was, however, fulsome and generous: 'I want to say, here and now, that Britten has been for me the most purely musical person that I have ever met and I have ever known. It always seemed to me that music sprang out of his fingers when he played the piano, as it did out of his mind when he composed.'[8] This didn't mean that he, like Britten in

[5] Christopher Grogan (ed.), *Imogen Holst: A Life in Music* (Woodbridge: Boydell Press, 2007), 150.
[6] BB 193.
[7] Michael Tippett, *Those Twentieth Century Blues: An Autobiography* (London: Hutchinson, 1991), 117.
[8] Reproduced in LL2 1154.

turn, didn't have criticisms. To Anna Kallin of the BBC he wrote, for example, in 1954, 'I come to think that a lot of the trouble with our minor English operatic attempts (including even a lot of B.B.) is timing; and insufficient struggle to solve the special problems.'[9] He was not overly impressed with *Peter Grimes*, writing to the poet Douglas Newton after the premiere:

> I should like you to see *Peter Grimes* sometime. It's obvious that the masque [Tippett's first opera, *The Midsummer Marriage* (1946–52), which he had started to plan] will be so different it's almost frightening. I mean that we shall risk a serious failure to please because of our story's marked unsentimentality and so on. *Grimes* is nothing if not properly romantic. The emotional situation is pictured all the time in the music (not the action or gesture) quite like *Tristan*, but with less power. Two scenes are very good, but a lot of it is rather disappointing.[10]

Some of this may simply be the result of Tippett's conception of opera being very different, as is apparent in this comment to Carpenter: 'I didn't like it personally, because it seemed to me a false statement. I thought, this is an English *verismo*, and I don't want to go down that road. I'm going into the world of magic.'[11] There is little doubt, though, that Tippett felt, certainly during the 1940s, that he was rather in the shadow of his younger colleague, whose public profile was much greater than his. He was also somewhat in Britten's debt: Britten had encouraged him in the composition of his oratorio, *A Child of Our Time* (1939–41), and secured him a commission for the Fanfare No. 1 for Brass (1943) for the festival at St Matthew's Church in Northampton (the festival for which Britten composed *Rejoice in the Lamb*). Britten also offered Tippett something of a haven on occasion: in 1944 he stayed in Britten and Pears's flat while his cottage was repaired,[12] and in 1950, during the composition of *The Midsummer Marriage*, he went 'to stay for a week (at least) with Britten, to have a complete rest, before [gathering himself] together to imagine the pre-final draft of Act 3'.[13]

It was with regard to the Fanfare that Tippett admitted, to William Glock in 1945, 'I was looked on as a sort of minor Ben ... I seem to have gone through some minor internal struggle and once for all relinquished competition in success as being foreign

[9] Schuttenhelm, *Selected Letters of Michael Tippett*, 366.
[10] Ibid., 183–4.
[11] *BB* 220.
[12] Schuttenhelm, *Selected Letters of Michael Tippett*, 178.
[13] Ibid., 25.

to my proper nature. But obviously I get momentary returnings and twinges of adolescent envy – only being me, it's all pretty mild!'[14] The Northampton Festival had taken place two years earlier, so the comparison with Britten evidently had a big effect. At the time he wrote to his close friend Francesca Allinson in similar tones saying that, at the Festival, 'I was B.B.'s "younger brother", asked to show "his" talent and promise – all out of B.B.'s unconscious and sincere desire to help me to win recognition. And because his, Ben's, enormous popularity and success has been making me try to force myself along at the same pace and towards the same ends.'[15]

It would seem that Britten was still eclipsing his older colleague in terms of public profile up to the early 1960s at least: after all, *War Requiem* garnered so much attention at the festival for the consecration of the new cathedral in Coventry that it is rarely remembered that Tippett's *King Priam* – his second opera, and a work that saw a crucial reorientation in terms of technique – was given its first performance at the festival the day before (29 May 1962). But as Britten appeared increasingly to withdraw into the Aldeburgh set-up, so Tippett began to move more centre-stage. Writing in an often scathingly critical piece marking Tippett's ninetieth birthday, Derrick Puffett observed, regarding the composers' relative positions, that 'Sometime in the mid-60s it all changed. After the first performance of Britten's *War Requiem* (1962) – a disappointment then, for many of those who loved his more intimate works, whatever one may think of it now – it seemed clear that Britten could no longer provide the example one wanted.'[16] Revivals of Tippett's *Midsummer Marriage* in 1963 and 1968, which Puffett goes on to mention, seem to have led to a critical rethinking of what had seemed a fatally muddled work, and therefore of Tippett in general; and the more secure performances that new generations of performers, more attuned to post-World War II compositional developments, could provide must have helped to clarify the strengths of Tippett's approach. But it is perhaps the last clause of the Puffett quotation that is most crucial: it was Tippett, whose music was more obviously engaged with modernism than Britten's, who became the figurehead for the younger generation. Thus it was Tippett who was asked to be president of the Wardour Castle Summer Schools

[14] Ibid., 257.
[15] Ibid., 111.
[16] Derrick Puffett, 'Tippett and the Retreat from Mythology', *The Musical Times*, 136 (Jan. 2001), 7.

that took place in 1964 and 1965. He was the only composer of his generation present. Initiated by Harrison Birtwistle and led by him and Peter Maxwell Davies and Alexander Goehr (who were billed as the 'musical directors'), the Schools were attended by a roll call of emerging British talent.[17] Tippett's music was represented by his recent Piano Sonata No. 2 (1962) – the most radical of his work to that date in its embrace of mosaic form and sidelining of traditional notions of harmony and tonality – and the less recent *Little Music* for strings (1946); he also introduced concerts and participated in composition classes.

No doubt Tippett's sheer accessibility as a person, as well as the working relationship he had forged with Walter Goehr, Alexander's father, played a part in the creation of this role. But there was another draw-card, too. In 1959 Tippett had published a series of essays, *Moving into Aquarius*,[18] and while these might have seemed a little tangential to the kind of progressiveness most of the composers who attended the Schools were interested in, theirs was a stance that (as in the more rarified summer school at Darmstadt) went hand in hand with theoretical debate. Tippett was the first major English composer to declare himself as an intellectual with interests in a wide range of subjects. Britten ventured his thoughts on diverse matters in interviews from the beginning of the 1960s, but he steered clear of theoretical discussion except in the most general terms, and rarely spoke or wrote about non-musical subjects.

As it happens, Tippett rarely engaged with technical matters in specific terms, either, and a knowledge of the actual music of both composers might lead to the conclusion that, while Tippett was an intellectual in the general sense, Britten was the 'musical intellectual', revelling in the setting and solving of compositional problems and the display of a virtuosic compositional technique (which is by no means at odds with writing music for amateurs and children). For Tippett it seems that music was the carrier, rather than the domain itself – the means by which a door is opened onto a visionary realm. For Britten, music was the ultimate condition.

---

[17] See Michael Hooper's extensive documentation and interviews at <http://wardourcastlesummerschool.wordpress.com>.
[18] Michael Tippett, *Moving into Aquarius* (Frogmore, St Albans: Paladin, 1974).

FIVE

INFIRMITY, DEATH (1972–1976)

It was while Britten was working on his final opera, *Death in Venice*, Op. 88 (1973), based on a novella by Thomas Mann,[1] that it became clear that he was going to need an operation to repair the degradation of a heart valve. He had a check-up at around the time he was conducting a recording of Schumann's *Faust*, a project that clearly took a lot out of him. He agreed with his doctor that he would reduce his commitments to save his energy for composing, and await full treatment until after *Death in Venice* was finished; in the interim his condition would be treated with drugs.[2] Britten later explained to Alan Blyth:

> I wanted passionately to finish this piece before anything happened. For one thing, it is probably Peter's last major operatic part; for another, it was an opera I had been thinking about for a very long time, and it had already been postponed once. I had to keep going, and then, when I had finished, put myself in the doctors' hands … I was quite ready for [an operation], because I felt very bad. But work is a funny thing, and while I was still busy on the opera I had good days, and forgot about my condition. But I did feel rotten, and unable to go up stairs without stopping on the way. And there is no doubt that working on such a huge score as *Death in Venice* was extremely exhausting.[3]

The operation took place two months after *Death in Venice* was completed, on 7 May 1973, and was a success only in a very limited sense: it appears that, in the words of one of Britten's consultants, during surgery 'certain bits of debris from the valve entered the circulation and one lodged in his brain' and this led to some restriction of mobility on his right side.[4] The

---

[1] A famous film version by Visconti was released in 1971 while Britten was writing the opera, but was deliberately avoided by the composer.
[2] *BB* 543.
[3] Alan Blyth, 'Britten Returns to Composing', *The Times*, 30 Dec. 1974.
[4] *BB* 549.

operation had also failed to restore the proper functioning of the valve, leaving Britten permanently weakened.

Given the composer's aesthetic imperative of ensuring that his music was 'pruned and pruned and pruned'[5], there is a bitter irony in his being forced because of illness to reduce his activity to 'mere' composition, stripping away the performing and administration that were no less significant to what he wanted to achieve, if ultimately ancillary. But composition was affected, too: physical incapacity meant he had to write fewer notes; reduced stamina necessitated compact forms. For all that, the post-*Death in Venice* music was not noticeably that of an incapacitated man.

Ambiguous Venice

The first performance of *Death in Venice* took place in Britten's absence on 16 June that year. Like *Peter Grimes* and *War Requiem*, it can be thought of as a nodal point in Britten's output. It too is a big, highly ambitious statement that draws on a wide range of techniques and contains a breadth of references to external musical resources as well as Britten's own immediate (and in the case of this work, fairly distant) musical past. It could be argued that it is the most ambitious of all his works. Britten himself indicated a degree of trepidation in a letter of 6 January 1971 to John Piper – again the set designer: '… I do hope to write very soon & suggest a plan for Venetian discussion (I feel so nervous about even mentioning the name of the new opera!)' (*LL6* 406), while Piper's wife, Myfanwy – again the librettist – had acknowledged the challenges a few months earlier (11 September 1970): 'I've thought a lot about Death in Venice & read it again. Its [*sic*] a wonderful idea – a very difficult one but I look forward immensely to tackling it. I think it a perfect subject for you at the moment and I think, by its nature, it will be quite unlike any other operatic work' (*BPL*). Not the least significant challenge was how to present the thoughts and reactions of the protagonist, the 'famous writer' Gustav von Aschenbach. Colin Graham – again the producer – offered some thoughts sometime in 1971 (the letter is not dated):

> Ever since you said 'Death in Venice' the idea has haunted me and I hope you won't mind being presented with my thoughts on the subject. If you are no longer interested, then forget the whole thing. The enclosed is not a libretto, but suggestions for a scheme for adaptation of the book to an opera – a blue-print, as it were, of the practicalities, how I see it could be done – even in Snape! (*BPL*)

Graham goes on to observe that, in such an adaptation, 'two difficulties seem to be supreme: one, how to adapt for singing a book in which the

---

[5] The words Britten used when interviewed by a *Guardian* journalist: see *BB* 536.

protagonists never address a single word to each other & in which most of the thoughts are unspoken. Two, how to provide a plan that will not be humanly insufferable – vocally & stamina-wise, for the leading gent!' He proposed two stages, A and B – stage A was to be Aschenbach's 'brain-world', stage B was to be for the action scenes 'and is also very useful for distancing Gustav from Tadzio, the unattainable, by putting them on two different planes'. Finally, in a PS, he suggested that 'It would be a marvellous idea to exploit the different dimensions of speech & song when used in extended sections – with or without orchestral backing.'

He was certainly right about the taxing nature of the role for the 'leading gent' (Pears, of course, aged 62 when he created the part), who is on stage for virtually the entire opera. Scarcely less taxing is the role for the baritone who plays a number of characters who seem to be conveying Aschenbach towards his fate. The concept of two stages doesn't seem to have been taken up, the distinction between Aschenbach's and Tadzio's worlds being enacted in the end by having Tadzio and his family played by non-singing dancers; the 'otherness' of the latter is embodied musically by a gamelan-like sound-world. The suggested distinction between speech and song was taken up, however, with Aschenbach's 'brain-world' reflections (the 'Performance and Production Notes' in the score refers to these as 'interior monologues') being undertaken in recitative. The ambition of the enterprise is further indicated by Britten's comment in October 1972 to Frederick Ashton (who choreographed the 'Games of Apollo' in Scene 7) that the opera was 'either the best or the worst music I've ever written'.[6] The most daring aspect, though, one might think, was the subject-matter, which broaches aspects of Britten's personality in a remarkably public way.

The story at its most basic involves an ageing writer, Gustav von Aschenbach, very aware of his eminence, seeking the rejuvenation of his parched creative forces by taking a trip to Venice. He becomes increasingly obsessed with a beautiful Polish boy, Tadzio, with whom he has only visual exchanges. In his desire to make speaking contact with him he pursues him and his family through Venice. Immediately before the pursuit Aschenbach hears of a cholera outbreak in the city, and becomes anxious, first that the family 'must not leave', and then that they should 'go away at once'. Disgusted at his inability to speak to Tadzio's mother ('So I didn't speak! Once again I have failed to make ev'rything decent and above board, missed the opportunity to become myself again') and by the nature of his obsession ('I can fall no further'), he dies on the beach as Tadzio walks out to sea and beckons to him.

---

[6] BB 545.

17. *Aschenbach (Peter Pears) gazes at the victorious Tadzio (Bryan Pitts) during the Games of Apollo in the New York Metropolitan Opera production of* Death in Venice *(October 1974).*

Parallels between Aschenbach and Britten are such that it is impossible not to see the opera as being in some way autobiographical. They are both honoured artists working under the weight of public expectation; 'self-discipline [is their] strength' and 'Routine the order of [their] day'; they both focus obsessively on work; their work displays an emphasis on simplicity; they both 'welcomed the demands of maturity' (in Britten's case he might not actually have welcomed them, but he accepted them); and they both have a love of the sea. There are differences, too: there's no sign, for example, that Britten had dried up creatively, which is Aschenbach's lot at the beginning of the opera. It would therefore be misguided to assume that Aschenbach essentially is Britten – not least because Britten is embodied to a certain extent in Tadzio, too. But there is one particular aspect of the story – Aschenbach's developing obsession with the 14-year-old Tadzio – that demands careful consideration.

The common view of Britten's *Death in Venice* is that it is essentially about a conflict between the Apollonian and the Dionysian. This comes to a head in Scene 13, a dream sequence in which the voices of Apollo (at Pears's suggestion, the other-worldly timbre of a countertenor) and Dionysus (sung by the baritone in multiple roles) compete for Aschenbach's acquiescence. It is clear, though, that the balance is already tipped firmly in Dionysus' favour, since he has the first say in the scene, and is introduced by the more lush, inviting orchestral music – warm strings, moving upwards with increasing intensity on each iteration. This music is associated with Aschenbach's decision in the opera's first scene to 'pursue this freedom and offer up my days to the sun and the south'; Apollo's music is less purposefully directed. Apollo is entirely on the defensive, each response (to Dionysus' 'Reject the abyss', 'Love reason, beauty, form', and so on) beginning with 'No!'. The ensuing Dionysian dance that celebrates the triumph is a variation of Tadzio's music, suggesting the mutual dependency of the two sides. We know this already, though. Aschenbach tries to cover his initial reaction to Tadzio with a nonchalant response (as Mann puts it, '"Good, oh, very good indeed"', thought Aschenbach, assuming the patronizing air of the connoisseur to hide, as artists will, their ravishment over a masterpiece'), but the audience isn't fooled: the listener's response to the sound of Tadzio's theme is surely to find it suggestively alluring.

No control, no art; no abandonment, no artistic impulse: this is the dichotomy that forms the basis for Aschenbach's final 'brain-world' scene, which is enacted through the lens of Plato's *Phaedrus*. Exhausted mentally and physically, Aschenbach finds himself driven into an impasse. As Evans observes, 'All that can remain in the drama is the hopeless playing-out'[7] of Aschenbach's leave-taking: the setting of the text 'And now Phaedrus, I

---

7   Peter Evans, *The Music of Benjamin Britten* (2nd edn, London: Dent, 1989), 533.

will go. But you stay here and when your eyes no longer see me, then you go, too' is an arch of simple, unaccompanied melody that is extraordinarily affecting.

But is it possible to regard the opera simply as an abstract discourse that uses burgeoning lust for a boy as a mere starting-point? The phrase 'What if all were dead and only we two left alive', delivered twice, the second time just before the Socrates 'aria' (these are arguably Aschenbach's only moments of complete self-awareness), makes it clear that it is Aschenbach's obsession for Tadzio's physical being, not just his abstracted beauty, that has come to possess him. Joan Cross, the first Ellen Orford, described *Death in Venice* to Carpenter as 'preaching to the converted', which Carpenter understood as meaning that it was 'a celebration of paedophilia intended for the delight of fellow initiates'.[8] Trying to make sense of Britten's opaque comment to Donald Mitchell that '*Death in Venice* is everything that Peter and I have stood for', Carpenter takes Mitchell's line that Britten is referring to 'the obligatory consequential restraints, the absence of which ... was ultimately Aschenbach's undoing' and concludes that the work is 'an anguished autobiography by Britten, an account of the tension and guilt he had experienced because of his feelings for boys; also an *apologia pro vita sua* which answers those who ... had assumed the worst of him'.[9]

Clifford Hindley follows a different line, suggesting that if Aschenbach had been able to make contact with Tadzio and 'engage creatively with the reality before him', 'an open friendship with [him] might have brought to fruition the hopes for artistic renewal which had led him to Venice'.[10] From here one might go on to ask whether the opera could be thought of as Britten's rebuff to Auden's letter of January 1942 (the poet was still alive while Britten was writing the work but died soon after the first performance) – especially, given Britten's escalating health problems, Auden's suggestion in that letter that Britten's 'denial and evasion of the demands of disorder' – the middle-class Englishman's propensity for 'Bourgeois convention' – had led to his attacks of ill-health, that 'sickness [was his] substitute for the Bohemian'.

How listeners interpret this deeply ambiguous work, which is perhaps the pinnacle of ambiguity in an œuvre that is much consumed with it, is likely to depend on what they make of the orchestral music that concludes the opera after Aschenbach has slumped in his chair, 'At a clear beckon from Tadzio' (as it says in the stage instructions). If the opera up to this point is beheld almost entirely through Aschenbach's eyes, the ending is surely a narrative comment (he is dead or dying – the precise moment of

---

[8] BB 552–3.
[9] BB 552, 553.
[10] Clifford Hindley, 'Eros in Life and Death: *Billy Budd* and *Death in Venice*', in Mervyn Cooke (ed.), *The Cambridge Companion to Benjamin Britten* (Cambridge: Cambridge University Press, 1999), 157–8.

death is not clear). The music here is a reworking of Aschenbach's Hymn to Beauty, which he had sung at the height of his intellectual justification of his reaction to Tadzio, and which is now counterpointed by Tadzio's music. The two strands finally come to rest on the same highpoint, the final note. Is this a sublimation achieved finally in death? Or a representation of an ideal that ultimately lies beyond Aschenbach's grasp?

Whatever one decides the essential message of *Death in Venice* is, the work must be counted as one of Britten's most impressive musical achievements. The wide range of resources used includes the 'controlled floating' and heterophony of the Church Parables, aspects of twelve-tone serialism, a transcription of the Ancient Greek First Delphic Hymn, and gondoliers' cries and Italian popular song (which Britten notated during his visits to Venice). The intercutting from Aschenbach's 'brain-world' to the 'real' world and the requirement to have short scenes in succession led to Britten's development of the musical equivalent of filmic dissolves, and a mode of continuity derived from his film-music and recent television-opera experiences. One scene for which this is especially important is Aschenbach's pursuit of Tadzio through the streets of Venice. This is set as a passacaglia – the series of variations built on a repeating bass theme is something of a Britten calling-card (all his operas contain one) – and it works, fairly obviously but no less effectively for that, as a symbol of obsession; as Aschenbach says, 'Yet am I driven on.'

'A marvellous therapy'

After his heart operation Britten made revisions to *Paul Bunyan* and another work that had not been published, a String Quartet in D from 1931, as a way of easing himself back into composition. In his interview for Alan Blyth's *Times* article he describes coming to terms with his situation and the initial difficulties he faced:

> 'I have now accepted the situation. It has become a *modus vivendi*. I can't look after myself. Getting about has become extremely difficult. But I can write.
>
> 'For a time after the operation I couldn't compose because I had no confidence in my powers of selection. I was worried too about my ideas. Then I suddenly got my confidence back about five months ago, and now composing has become, apart from anything else, a marvellous therapy. Now that I can write again, I have the feeling of being of some use once more ... What gets me back on the rails again is working. As Ian [Tait, his doctor] says, psychologically that seems important. Whether it is musically' – and here some of the old Britten humour came back – 'only time will tell'.[11]

---

[11] Alan Blyth, 'Britten Returns to Composing', *The Times*, 30 Dec. 1974.

Getting back to composing was all the more crucial because Pears was not ready to retire and continued to have engagements that took him away for long stretches – not only for Covent Garden and overseas performances of *Death in Venice* but also concerts and masterclasses that, arguably, could have been postponed to allow him to remain at home and support his partner. Pears seems (at times, at least) to have been in denial about the seriousness of Britten's condition,[12] and undertook a trip to Los Angeles and Toronto in November 1976 when, according to Donald Mitchell's wife, Kathleen, 'It was clear that Ben was dying from the end of October when he came back from Horham to take to his bed at the Red House. Those of us who saw him at that time knew how desperately he wanted Peter to be with him.'[13] Pears's biographer, Christopher Headington, observes that

> Later Pears was to say, 'My regret is that I did not spend more time with him in those last months of his life'. But he never explained why he failed to do so, when he must have known that these months were perhaps the last that he and Britten could share. It may be that his lifelong tendency to avoid difficult situations worked here as so often elsewhere. But in this particular instance, even those who loved him most found him hard to understand.[14]

There is testimony that Pears had a number of affairs around this time. Britten apparently took the attitude of 'I don't care what Peter gets up to providing I don't know about it'.[15] Although there were periods when Pears was with Britten, including holidays spent together with friends, the

18. *Britten on the sea near Bergen, Norway, during his last holiday, July 1976.*

[12] See, for example, *BB* 561 and 569, in which he is reported as allowing Britten to carry luggage, saying, 'I find it terribly hard to judge how important Ben's ups and down's [*sic*] are.'
[13] Christopher Headington, *Peter Pears: A Biography* (London: Faber & Faber, 1992), 272.
[14] Ibid., 273.
[15] *BB* 570.

composer's main companion during his final two years was Rita Thomson, a former senior sister at the National Heart Hospital who joined the Red House staff to nurse him.

The works Britten completed in 1974 and 1975 are either relatively short or consist of a number of short movements, but they do not lack in musical punch and emotional power. Perhaps by way of preparation for his own exit, most of them are concerned with death – *Canticle V: The Death of St Narcissus*, Op. 89 (completed July 1974) for voice and harp; *Sacred and Profane*, Op. 91 (January 1975) for chamber choir; and *Phaedra*, Op. 93 (August 1975), a dramatic cantata for mezzo-soprano and small orchestra – or with loss, as at the end of the orchestral *Suite on English Folk Tunes 'A Time There Was'*, Op. 90 (November 1974), the subtitle quoting from the Hardy poem Britten set as the last song of *Winter Words*, Op. 52 (1954).

A special case is the String Quartet No. 3, Op. 94 (composed in Venice, November 1975), since the last of its five movements – Britten's final passacaglia – makes direct reference to *Death in Venice*, quoting from it and revolving around the key associated with Aschenbach in the opera, E major. One has to say 'revolving around' E major rather than 'in' it because of the remarkable way in which the movement – and therefore the work – finishes. It is certainly an ending, clearly marked as such rhetorically. It is also profoundly satisfying. But there is no closure: the final chord, while containing elements of the tonic chord, is conspicuously 'not-tonic' as an entity, with the most clearly not-tonic note, the low D natural in the cello, being sustained into silence after the others have already faded. Britten is reputed to have said that he wished the work to end with a question, but a less prosaic way of describing the effect (and certainly better than saying that the ending is 'conflicted') might be that the need for closure is transcended.

In his first aria delivered in Venice, in a gondola on the way to his hotel on the Lido, Aschenbach sings of 'Ambiguous Venice'. The fluidity of the quartet's first movement seems an embodiment of this: harmonically, it has no stable ground, and the normal boundaries between 'statements' and 'things-done-to-statements' (development or variation or transformation) are shadowy, too – one could argue that in fact there aren't any statements. The sardonic second and fourth movements contain the work's most Dionysian music. The third movement, perhaps the most remarkable of them all, is the heart of the quartet. The first violin traces a serene arc of melody while the lower instruments slowly move through ascending arpeggiations of simple triads. The achievement, or distillation, of pure C major at the end of the movement is the 'highest' Apollonian moment in the work, and possibly in Britten's output.

String Quartet No. 3 received its first performance at Snape Maltings on 19 December 1976. Britten had died fifteen days before, during the early hours of 4 December. Pears was at his bedside, holding his hand.

19. *Snape Maltings, from the back, photographed in June 2004.*

Epilogue

Britten had been awarded a life peerage in June during the 1976 Aldeburgh Festival. It is difficult to know what to make of his acceptance of it. Rosamund Strode reported that the composer 'just felt it was marvellous for music',[16] which seems a standard meaningless deflection. Philip Brett seems close to the mark when he observes that 'Others have viewed his acceptance with puzzlement or irony: but it seems entirely characteristic of the man who wanted so much to belong to the society he thought he didn't fit into.'[17]

Following Britten's death there was the inevitable tidying up in the obituaries. *The Times* (which printed its notice next to a piece entitled 'The Christian dilemma over homosexuality', whether by intention or accident we shall never know) was generally warm, as it had been towards Britten's music all through his last decade or so.[18] Suggesting that 'He was the first British composer to capture and hold the attention of musicians and their audiences the world over, as well as at home', the obituary emphasized Britten's professionalism and rigour – 'The famous dictum, "Only connect", of E. M. Forster ... finds an outstanding example in the personality and work of Britten; everything that he did ... had some intelligible, logical relevance to his personal faith and idealism' – as well as his adherence to the credo set out in this book's Introduction: 'rarely have such artistic

---

[16] BB 580.
[17] BBGO.
[18] 'Lord Britten: a Major Contribution to English Music', *The Times*, 6 Dec. 1976.

endowments been matched with such a sense of human responsibility for their best use.'

The piece in *The Musical Times*, by its editor, Stanley Sadie, was more circumspect.[19] It began by stating that 'His views, on life and on music, were progressive, anti-authoritarian, and actuated by strong humane feelings'. Identifying *Grimes* as 'his greatest opera', it questioned 'Whether our sympathies are handled fairly', but recognized that they are 'handled powerfully; and the opera's evocations of sea and shore and the people that inhabit them remain without peer'. Sadie ventures criticism of both *A Midsummer Night's Dream* ('a highly characteristic and individual score, yet arguably too exquisite and too miniature in a very English way to have much long-term impact') and *Owen Wingrave* ('with its unchanged theme of empty-headed belligerence and cruel victimization of the individual, [this] seemed to break little new ground and to suggest a simplistic handling of certain of the issues') before offering a summarizing statement:

> That Britten occupies a place in British music alongside Elgar and Vaughan Williams, and as their successor, is not in question. He has traditional English qualities: a certain pragmatic conservatism of idiom, a deep sensitivity to poetry and especially to its melancholy side, a freshness of melody and lucidity of texture, and a Protestant attitude to pain and redemption. Abroad he is less highly valued, possibly but not entirely because our poetry is less understood. It may be that those early scars [by which Sadie meant his being 'desperately unhappy at school, to the point of running away', which is, however, and mysteriously, 'only a part of it'] were too deep and too painful for him ever to absorb them and then to move on and rise above them; and that could only narrow any composer's range.

Both obituaries play safe. The praise and the criticism alike were hardly new and were studiedly uncontroversial, even if *The Musical Times*'s view of *A Midsummer Night's Dream* seems (from today's point of view, at least) somewhat eccentric.

Drawing on a longer perspective, and writing in the revised *New Grove Dictionary* of 2001 (though still working within the constraints of a self-consciously 'official' organ of opinion[20]), Philip Brett observes that in contrast to many composers immediately after their death, 'there was no appreciable lapse of interest in [Britten's] music; its audience rather increased during the last quarter of the 20th century.'[21] He goes on to speculate that 'Perhaps the tide that swept away serialism, atonality and

[19] *The Musical Times*, vol. 118, no. 1608 (Feb. 1977), 147–9.
[20] Brett's *New Grove* entry on gay and lesbian music, co-authored with Elizabeth Wood, was subject to heavy editorial intervention (see Susan McClary, 'Introduction' in Philip Brett, *Music and Sexuality in Britten* (Berkeley, CA: University of California Press, 2006)), suggesting that Brett was working in a context laden with strong ideas about what could be officially sanctioned.
[21] BBGO.

most forms of musical modernism and brought in neo-Romanticism, minimalism and other modes of expression involved with tonality carried with it renewed interest in composers who had been out of step with the times.' Brett is still, though, reluctant to assess Britten's stature, regarding comparisons as 'unseemly': he is content merely to say that 'Like most remarkable composers he was inimitable, possessed of a distinctive voice which renovated every aspect of the classical tonal tradition in which he worked, a voice and sound too dangerous to imitate.'

It is certainly the case that comparisons need clear criteria if they are to be of any value, and that these are difficult to establish when – particularly in the century in which Britten worked – compositional ideologies and motivations were so various. And the reluctance to assess doesn't apply just to Britten: the critical ideology of post-modernism, which questions the stability of any ground on which assessment might be made, doesn't encourage the imputation of value. But in so-called ordinary listeners and concert-goers there doesn't seem to be a departure from the attitude, however distrusted it might be in the academy, that comparisons are the basic way in which we grasp the essence and significance of things – that debating the relative values of outputs, works and performances is one of the most pleasurable aspects of our musical culture, especially when we acknowledge the provisionality of our conclusions, thereby allowing ourselves to go through the whole pleasurable process again.

Surveying English music of the long twentieth century, one can revel in the sustained achievements of Elgar, Vaughan Williams, Walton, Tippett, Maxwell Davies and Birtwistle, and savour the peaks of the less consistent figures such as Warlock, Bridge, Rawsthorne or Lutyens (the list is necessarily selective, given the flowering of English composition at this time). But one might strongly argue that Britten has no equal among immediately preceding and contemporary English composers – and indeed those who have followed – with regard to consistency of quality of invention, and that his best music inhabits realms of imagination and technical resource beyond any other English composer since Purcell. From an international perspective it would appear that Britten's work has had little of the historical impact of, say, Stravinsky or the Second Viennese School or post-World War II radicals such as Boulez and Stockhausen: he was simply not the sort of composer who uprooted long-held compositional practices. He is, though, accorded a whole chapter to himself in Richard Taruskin's *Oxford History of Western Music*,[22] a history which seeks to shift that which is deemed historically significant away from an exclusive, teleologically driven focus on the 'progression' of compositional technique

---

[22] Richard Taruskin, *The Oxford History of Western Music*, 5 vols (2nd edn, Oxford; New York: Oxford University Press, 2010), vol. 5 'Music in the Late Twentieth Century', chap. 5 'Stand-off I: Music in Society: Britten', 221–60.

to include cultural and social forces, including audience reception. By these lights Britten's significance would seem to be as high as any in the twentieth century. In any case, his music does not lack the ambition or vision that a composer intent on making an impact on musical history might be expected to show. And it might be argued that his attempt to offer listeners a rewarding, engaging experience of the musically new by building on and transforming traditional musical elements and procedures is more ambitious than the avant-garde's *tabula rasa* approach.

Meanwhile the topics of his operas and other sung works have proved to have been of continuing significance: *pace* Sadie, English geographical setting and English texts have not, in fact, proved a barrier to international enthusiasm. Though more recent composers, particularly those associated with minimalism and post-minimalism, have sometimes achieved large audiences, no subsequent 'classical' work has replicated the impact of *War Requiem*, and one wonders, surveying the reports of dwindling classical-music audiences, whether this will now be possible. And whatever the response of later generations of composers to that work, they would surely agree with one of two major English composers born in the year of the first performance of *A Boy was Born*, Peter Maxwell Davies,[23] who wrote to Britten on a postcard from New York on the day he died:

> Dear Ben,
>
> On tour with the 'Fires of London' – doing my own music all over the USA & Canada, & other younger British composers. It occurs to me how impossible all this would have been without you – without the precedent you set, the wonderful sound world created!
>
> Much love,
>
> Peter Maxwell Davies. (*BPL*)

That Britten's music is rewarding and engaging for professional players to sing and play is not the least important factor in ensuring the prospects for his music's longevity. New generations of tenors have taken up the works written for Pears, new ensembles have taken up the quartets, and new productions of his operas continue to be made (and old ones revived). Uniquely among major twentieth-century composers, Britten composed a substantial body of work for amateurs and children to perform; that this is played less today than when he was alive might say more about the changing priorities and tastes of music educationalists than about the quality of the music.

The Festival he co-founded, and of which he was the driving force, continues to thrive – and to expand its purview, welcoming in 2010 Pierre Boulez (ostensibly as different a composer as is imaginable) to conduct his

---

23 The other was Harrison Birtwistle.

Ensemble Intercontemporain in a programme of works far from Britten's sympathies. How Britten would have reacted to this is impossible to say, but despite some strong ideological differences he might have seen in Boulez a kind of fellow traveller in the terms of his 1941 essay, 'England and the Folk-Art Problem': 'It is only those who accept their loneliness and refuse all the refuges … who will carry on the human heritage.'[24] Different kinds of refuge were in the event necessary for Britten, but there was none from the pursuit of professional duty – ruthlessly undertaken with respect to himself, first and foremost – that underpins his legacy.

20. *The 50 pence coin commissioned by the Royal Mint to mark the centenary of Britten's birth on 22 November 2013; designed by Tom Phillips, the coin features Tennyson's words set by Britten in* Serenade *for tenor, horn and strings, and is the first British coin to be issued in celebration of a composer.*

---

[24] *BoM* 35.

References

Banks, Paul (ed.), *The Making of Peter Grimes: Essays and Studies* (Woodbridge: Boydell Press, 2000).

Blyth, Alan, *Remembering Britten* (London: Hutchinson, 1981).

Brett, Philip, *Benjamin Britten: Peter Grimes* (Cambridge: Cambridge University Press, 1983).

——, *Music and Sexuality in Britten* (Berkeley, CA: University of California Press, 2006).

——et al., 'Britten, Benjamin', in *Grove Music Online*, http://www.oxfordmusiconline.com/subscriber/article/grove/music/46435

Bridcut, John, *Britten's Children* (London: Faber & Faber, 2006).

——, *The Faber Pocket Guide to Britten* (London: Faber & Faber, 2010).

Carpenter, Humphrey, *Benjamin Britten: A Biography* (London: Faber & Faber, 1992).

Cooke, Mervyn, *Benjamin Britten: War Requiem* (Cambridge: Cambridge University Press, 1996).

——, *Britten and the Far East* (Woodbridge: Boydell Press and The Britten-Pears Library, 1997).

——(ed.), *The Cambridge Companion to Benjamin Britten* (Cambridge: Cambridge University Press, 1999).

Duncan, Ronald, *Working with Britten: A Personal Memoir* (Welcombe: The Rebel Press, 1981).

Evans, John (ed.), *Journeying Boy: The Diaries of the Young Benjamin Britten 1928–1938* (London: Faber & Faber, 2009).

Evans, John, Philip Reed and Paul Wilson (eds.), *A Britten Source Book* (Aldeburgh: The Britten Estate, 1987).

Evans, Peter, 'Britten's "War Requiem"', *Tempo*, 61/2 (1962), 20–24; 29–39.

——, *The Music of Benjamin Britten* (2nd edn, London: Dent, 1989).

Grogan, Christopher (ed.), *Imogen Holst: A Life in Music* (Woodbridge: Boydell Press, 2007).

Harper-Scott, J. P. E., *Elgar: An Extraordinary Life* (London: ABRSM, 2007).

Headington, Christopher, *Peter Pears: A Biography* (London: Faber & Faber, 1992).

Hindley, Clifford, 'Eros in life and death: "Billy Budd" and "Death in Venice"', in Mervyn Cooke (ed.), *The Cambridge Companion to Benjamin Britten* (Cambridge: Cambridge University Press, 1999), 147–66.

Holloway, Robin, *On Music: Essays and Diversions* (Brinkworth: Claridge Press, 2003).

Kildea, Paul, *Selling Britten* (Oxford: Oxford University Press, 2002).

——(ed.), *Britten on Music* (New York: Oxford University Press, 2003).

LeGrove, Judith, 'Aldeburgh', in Mervyn Cooke (ed.), *The Cambridge Companion to Benjamin Britten* (Cambridge: Cambridge University Press, 1999), 306–17.

Mark, Christopher, 'Simplicity in Early Britten', *Tempo*, 147 (1983), 8–14.

——, 'Juvenilia (1922–1932)', in Mervyn Cooke (ed.), *The Cambridge Companion to Benjamin Britten* (Cambridge: Cambridge University Press, 1999), 11–35.

Mitchell, Donald, *Britten and Auden in the Thirties* (London: Faber & Faber, 1981).

Mitchell, Donald and Hans Keller (eds.), *Benjamin Britten: A Commentary on his Works from a Group of Specialists* (London: Rockcliffe, 1952).

Mitchell, Donald and Philip Reed (eds.), *Letters from a Life: Selected Diaries and Letters of Benjamin Britten. Volume 1 1923–39* (London: Faber & Faber, 1991).

—— (eds.), *Letters from a Life: Selected Letters and Diaries of Benjamin Britten. Volume 2 1939–45* (London: Faber & Faber, 1991).

Mitchell, Donald, Philip Reed and Mervyn Cooke (eds.), *Letters from a Life: Selected Letters of Benjamin Britten. Volume 3 1946–51* (London: Faber & Faber, 2004).

Palmer, Christopher (ed.), *The Britten Companion* (London: Faber & Faber, 1984).

Puffett, Derrick, 'Tippett and the Retreat from Mythology', *The Musical Times*, 136 (Jan. 2001), 6–14.

Reed, Philip (ed.), *The Travel Diaries of Peter Pears 1936–1978* (Woodbridge: Boydell & Brewer, 1995).

Reed, Philip, Mervyn Cooke and Donald Mitchell (eds.), *Letters from a Life: Selected Letters of Benjamin Britten. Volume 4 1952–1957* (Woodbridge: Boydell Press, 2008).

Reed, Philip and Mervyn Cooke (eds.), *Letters from a Life: The Selected Letters of Benjamin Britten. Volume 5 1958–1965* (Woodbridge: Boydell Press, 2010).

—— (eds.), *Letters from a Life: The Selected Letters of Benjamin Britten. Volume 6 1966–1976* (Woodbridge: Boydell Press, 2012).

Schuttenhelm, Thomas (ed.), *Selected Letters of Michael Tippett* (London: Faber & Faber, 2005).

Seymour, Claire, *The Operas of Benjamin Britten: Expression and Evasion* (Woodbridge: Boydell & Brewer, 2004).

Taruskin, Richard, *The Oxford History of Western Music*, 5 vols (2nd edn, Oxford; New York: Oxford University Press, 2010).

Tippett, Michael, *Moving into Aquarius* (Frogmore, St Albans: Paladin, 1974).

——, *Those Twentieth Century Blues: An Autobiography* (London: Hutchinson, 1991).

Tippins, Sherill, *February House* (London: Pocket Books, 2005).

Walker, Lucy (ed.), *Benjamin Britten: New Perspectives on his Life and Work* (Woodbridge: Boydell Press, 2009).

Wallace, Helen, *Boosey & Hawkes: The Publishing Story* (London: Boosey & Hawkes, 2007).

Whittall, Arnold, '"Twisted Relations": Method and Meaning in Britten's "Billy Budd"', *Cambridge Opera Journal*, 2/2 (1990), 145–71.

Wilcox, Michael, *Benjamin Britten's Operas* (Bath: Absolute Press, 1997).

Index